Strugglehood

A Practical Guide to Financial Situations No One Bothered Teaching Us

by
Brandon Brumage

For my wife.
There's zero chance this happened without you,
and
to our dear friend, AAH, may he rest in peace.

Table of Contents

Introduction

We all reach a point in our lives when we're finally on our own; yet, somehow, we're barely holding it together. This, my friends, is what I call Strugglehood. Have you come to the realization that you weren't properly prepared for some financial situations in your life? Does managing credit cards or paying taxes have you totally confused? Are you struggling to save money and pay off debts? Ever find yourself wondering what a 401(k) actually is? These thoughts are all too common nowadays. That's all about to change. End the struggle and become financially educated! #endthestrugglehood

We all grew up hearing the same redundant cliché phrases: "There's more to life than money," and, "Money doesn't buy happiness." Although these are true statements, essentially, money does make the world go 'round. While there's more to life than money, understanding how to accumulate it and keep it is going to play a huge part in enjoying the other, finer things in life. Knowing how to manage and save all of your hard-earned money certainly is going to make you happier.

Your life doesn't have to revolve around money. However, in order to be successful, support a family, save money for retirement, and lead the life you desire, you do need to know a thing or two about basic finances.

So why aren't we taught these financial concepts in school? Why must we graduate (whether it's high school or college) and come to the sudden, and sometimes painful, realization that we don't know how to manage our money? Why are we left to learn by trial and error? I'm ready for a change! Are you?

This book is for everyone who's entered or is entering adulthood with absolutely no idea how to manage their personal finances.

Specifically, I'm talking about budgeting and saving, managing credit and debt, paying off student loans, planning for retirement, and paying/filing your taxes. These are concepts you encounter every single day. In this book, I give you simple ways to understand and control your finances. These aren't complex concepts, but typically, they're presented in a dry and difficult-to-understand fashion. That's what sets this book apart; I've taken these topics and made them easy to understand without boring you to death! It's what you *need* to know.

I spent most of my time in school studying health sciences and now have a career in the healthcare field. I'm not a financial advisor or even in the financial industry, **which is exactly why you want to read this book**. I'm not going to use a bunch of jargon or terminology that you won't understand. These concepts aren't going to be over your head. I've broken everything down into basic, easy-to-comprehend subject matter because that's how I had to learn it. I was tired of always feeling embarrassed or even hopeless when the topic of finance was mentioned. Almost immediately, the conversation would reach a point where I honestly didn't know what was being said. Terms like APR and 401(k) were tossed around. I would find myself smiling and nodding, not actually knowing what was happening around me, looking for a chance to change the subject. This doesn't have to happen to you. If it has already, that was the last time!

Let's face it, most of us aren't working in the financial or banking industry. If you are, you probably have a solid foundation of these topics and don't need to read this book (but thank you if you are). For those of you who didn't major in finance or accounting, this is the book for you!

Making the decision to read this book has already started to change your life. Never again will you feel like you don't understand how to manage your finances. This book gives you the power and knowledge to fully comprehend debt, retirement planning, taxes, and much more.

I promise that after reading this book, you'll feel more confident in controlling your finances. You'll no longer feel stressed out, embarrassed, or incompetent like I did so many times.

Don't wait any longer to read on! Social Security isn't waiting around for you! Retirement may not even be an option if you keep holding out. No one wants to work until the day they die! Each chapter provides easy-to-understand, insightful, and helpful tips that give you master control of your personal finances. Start now and be young enough to retire with more money saved than you ever dreamt possible!

It's my hope to make a difference in someone's life through the teachings in this book. Hopefully, that someone is you! We should never quit learning, especially when it comes to your finances. Most importantly, I want to thank you sincerely for buying and reading this book.

Chapter 1:
How Did This Happen?

I blame the eighth grade. It's easy to look back and blame our issues on our adolescent years, isn't it? Seriously though, I can pinpoint it to one particular day. On this fateful day, the children of the eighth grade were expected to select their five-year plan. In other words, I was to choose the path I wanted to study for the next five years. Ultimately, I was deciding my career as a fourteen-year-old boy. Seems logical.

A few days prior to what I'll call "selection day," I had a dermatology appointment to rectify some teenage acne issues. While sitting in the waiting room with my mom, we started talking about dermatologists and their line of work. My mom began to tell me, to the best of her knowledge, the types of issues dermatologists dealt with, the hours they worked (anyone ever hear of a dermatologist being on call?), and the amount of money they made. It all sounded really appealing to me.

Later that week, I found myself sitting in a classroom on selection day with a blank form in front of me. The question, "What do you want to be when you grow up" was staring me in the face. Naturally, the first thing that came to mind was my conversation with my mother a few days prior regarding dermatologists—more specifically, the amount of money they made. Boom! That was it; I was going to be a dermatologist—done. When's lunch?

For the next four years during high school, my classes were heavy in the health sciences. Rather than getting a broader education and exposing myself to numerous disciplines, I was pigeonholed into taking mostly science classes. High school goes by, and I graduate without ever having taken a business or finance class. That should be criminal!

College comes and goes, and it's more of the same. I was exposed to some accounting and economics classes, but none of them actually focused on personal finances for the individual. So, I found myself at my first job, filling out initial start paperwork, and realized I had no idea what I was doing. I didn't even hesitate to think about retirement options and certainly didn't ask about it in my interviews. Retirement was so far away; I had plenty of time to worry about it later. I was given a Form W-4 to fill out for tax withholdings (full disclosure, I didn't know it was for tax withholdings at the time). I just breezed through it, putting zero for everything, not knowing what I was actually doing.

Paperwork completed, I started working. My first paycheck comes, and I open it excitedly (I was new to the idea of direct deposit and didn't quite trust it. So, I received physical paychecks—call me old school). "Where the hell did all my money go!?" Uncle Sam had had his way with me and gave me a rude awakening to tax withholdings. Six months go by, and I'm finally getting the hang of this adulting thing—or so I thought. Now, it was time for my student loan grace period to end. I said to myself, "OMG, I'll be paying these loans off until I'm fifty years old! This is insane! How did I make it this far without receiving any kind of advice or education on this stuff!?"

Maybe some of that sounds familiar, or you've even experienced it yourself. I've discovered, over the years, that I'm not alone in feeling this way. Why do we pay tens or hundreds of thousands of dollars to receive a college education only to graduate and be left feeling helpless or incompetent when it comes to handling our finances? Even if you didn't go to college, there's a strong chance you received little education on these topics growing up. Why is that? What's going on in our education system that we don't make it a priority to ensure every student knows how to handle the basics of finance? In the next chapter, I tried to discover the answer to that question. I conducted research and interviewed numerous teachers from multiple states throughout the country to see if there was an overall theme as to why this is happening.

Chapter 2:

Why Isn't This Taught?

It's almost laughable when you consider some of the topics that are required in schools while financial education remains an elective course if it's even offered. Sex education is a class that comes to mind. I remember being in fifth grade, learning about the birds and the bees, and it continued almost every year after that. I practically received eight years of sex education while zero minutes were spent on any sort of financial education. When I graduated, I knew all about condoms, safe sex, STDs, and teenage pregnancies and nothing about savings accounts, credit cards, 401(k)s, or taxes. I'm not downplaying the importance of sex ed., but it feels a bit lopsided, no?

A poll conducted in 2014 by Standard and Poor's Ratings Services and Gallup revealed the United States ranks 14th in financial literacy.[1] The average household credit card debt is $15,654, while the average student loan debt is $46,597![2] It gets worse. A 2017 study conducted by GoBankingRates.com discovered 69% of adults have less than $1,000 in their savings. Even worse, it showed 39% of Americans have nothing saved, as in $0.[3] You guys, these are horrific numbers! Fortunately, you're reading this book and won't fall into those percentiles.

I reached out to teachers across the country to get their opinions on the matter. After all, they're at the forefront of the problem. I sent out a questionnaire regarding the topic of personal finance education in their schools. Based on the results I received, this is what I can tell you. To my surprise, all of the respondents said they *do* offer some sort of finance class at their school. However, almost all of the teachers said the class was an elective and not required for graduation. When asked why they believe the class isn't more widely taught (required), only two different answers were received out of all the responses: emphasis on standardized testing and/or lack of funding from the state. The one that jumps out the most is that teachers have to teach to the subjects that will be on these tests. These same standardized tests care more about absurd math problems or theories. For example, thank goodness you were asked, "If Becky is traveling south with a car full of watermelons at 65 mph and Rick is traveling north at 70 mph with a truck filled with passion fruit, who's older?" Or to quote my favorite meme of all time, "I'm so glad I learned about parallelograms in school; it's really helped me this parallelogram season."

Okay, some of that was pretty far-fetched, but you get my point. It saddens me to hear that these teachers work so hard only to have their hands tied in terms of what they can really teach. Every single one of them indicated they felt it should be taught in school. Furthermore, 100% of respondents said they felt personal finance should not only be taught, but it should be a requirement for graduation.

How about other countries, what are they doing? If we're 14th in financial literacy, obviously, some other countries teach differently than the U.S. As of 2014, the U.K. made personal finance mandatory throughout the school system.[4] China has now incorporated financial concepts into cartoon films for elementary school children. They've even dedicated the whole month of September to financial literacy! Financial education has been embedded in Australian curriculum since 2014. Russia has developed core teachings for financial literacy for grades 2-11.[5] I spoke with a friend of mine in Canada who has children in the school systems there. He told me a finance course is required for each year of high school, grades 9-12. As you can see, the U.S. has some catching up to do if we intend to better the financial literacy of our citizens—most importantly, our younger generations. Standardized testing has all but taken over American education. Something needs to change.

As for the funding issues, an entirely new class doesn't have to be created. Just tweak the current curriculum. Interest rates and compounding interest can be taught in math classes. In history classes, Alexander Hamilton's influence on present-day banking can be discussed (Hamilton created the first national bank and developed a federal system to collect taxes). Required computer classes can teach students how to create a budget through programs like Microsoft Excel. Geography classes could be used to show how taxes vary from state to state. I realize I'm not a teacher, and it's a lot easier said than done. However, these aren't drastic changes that require a total overhaul of the curriculum. So, if any of you are educators out there, let's get together and see if we can make something happen! Feel free to email me: Brandon@strugglehood.com.

I'll step down off my soapbox now. I think these are important concepts, and we need to do what we can to ensure we have a grasp of basic financial principles. So, what can we do? Continue to learn. Don't be afraid to ask questions or admit you don't understand something. Until financial education can be integrated into schools everywhere, we have to continue to seek the knowledge on our own. Fortunately for you, you've picked up this book. So, without further ado, let's get into the real reason you're reading it—to learn the basic building blocks of personal finance. Are you ready to gain control of your financial life and start saving more money than you ever thought you could?

Chapter 3:

Budgeting

Here we are: the meat and potatoes. This is the reason you bought this book—to learn the basic building blocks of personal finance. The following nine chapters are rich with information about savings and budgeting, credit and debt, student loans, retirement planning, and taxes. Almost everyone I've ever spoken with about these subjects says the same thing: "I feel like we aren't taught how to handle financial situations we encounter every day." Why do we continue to just learn by trial and error? We don't do that with any other aspects of our lives. We research things. We take classes. We receive training. Well, I'm changing that. I want you to stop making the same mistakes as so many before you and to finally be confident when making financial decisions that can potentially affect the rest of your life!

Money isn't everything. I know that. But, damn, having and controlling it makes life a hell of a lot easier. So, settle in, order a pizza, and crack open a beer or a bottle of wine. I'm going to break down personal finances and make it easy for you to become confident in handling *your* money.

And at the root of personal finances is the concept of budgeting...

What Is Budgeting?

When most people hear the word *budgeting,* they envision a restricted lifestyle in which they can't spend an extra penny. I'm here to tell you that doesn't have to be true. Creating a budget allows you to see where you're spending money and how much you're saving. It gives you the opportunity to work toward financial goals. The truth of the matter is if you don't set a monthly budget, then you're really just flying by the seat of your pants. Now that you're officially an adult, having responsibilities and being held accountable, this can be extremely detrimental.

Whether you're living paycheck to paycheck or making good money, creating a budget is useful. It allows you to become conscious of your actual spending versus what you should be spending (and consequently, what you *could be* saving). Budgeting lets you see where you're spending money unnecessarily. It affords you the opportunity to make adjustments, saving you money in the long run. It also allows you to work toward financial goals such as buying a home, paying off student loans, taking vacations, or getting that new pair of Jordans that just dropped.

The benefits of budgeting are seen in both the short and long term. In particular, you can see weekly, monthly, and even yearly spending habits. Measuring yearly spending gives greater perspective. This example may seem cliché, but it's cliché for a reason. Say you spend $5 every morning at Starbucks before work. This seems small and tolerable when thinking about the course of a single day. Stop and consider the weekly and yearly effects though. Your $5 daily Starbucks habit costs you $25 dollars a week. Doesn't seem terrible? Extrapolate that $25 out to account for the entire year, and you've spent $1,300 on your skinny soy vanilla latte. Starbucks thanks you for your patronage.

This concept has been used by companies for years. You've undoubtedly heard commercials or sales pitches exclaim, "Just six easy payments of $39.99!" By breaking the price down into smaller payments, you're more likely to tolerate the incremental spending compared to a single purchase of $240. They rely on you seeing the $39.99 on your statement and not realizing how much you're actually spending over time. Budgeting allows you to focus on your overall financial situation, and then make your decision on whether the purchase is worth the expense.

How to Create a Budget

I hope it's obvious that everyone would benefit from creating a budget. So, let's look at how to create one. Many different programs and templates are available to help you with the process. Specifically, two are Google Sheets (GS) and Microsoft Excel. Also, specialized apps will do practically everything for you, such as Mint or Goodbudget. Personally, I use a "monthly budget" template on GS because it's easily accessible from my phone and any computer. Best of all, it's free. GS holds me more accountable because I have to enter my spending, and it forces me to stay on top of it, which I like. Whereas with Mint, you link all of your accounts (checking, savings, credit cards, investments, etc.), and it will automatically create everything for you. I realize that sounds easier because you don't have to do anything other than link your accounts. However, speaking from experience, I found I quit looking at it after a while. Google Sheets requires a more active participation, which I think is better, especially if you're just beginning to budget. Regardless, pick one and make sure to stick with it. The important thing is that you're budgeting your money.

Since I use GS, I'll guide you through how to create a budget using it. As a reference, I've included a picture below of Google Sheets's monthly budget template so you can see how easy it is to use. Before starting on your personal budget, let's look at an example template. Even if you don't use this specific template, most budgeting programs or apps have a similar structure. Below, you'll find an example of a monthly budget from our new friend Lucy. Go ahead and take a closer look at Lucy's budget, and then I'll walk you through everything you're seeing.

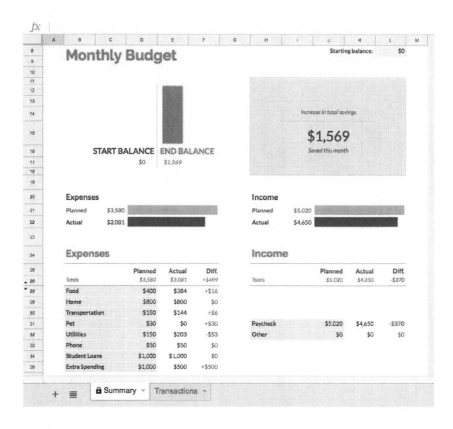

Lucy's budget is divided into two tabs that you see at the bottom of the picture—*Summary* and *Transactions*. As you can see, we're looking at the Summary tab. The first thing you'll probably notice is the start and end balance graph. The starting balance is a number that Lucy input (top right-hand corner). I recommend making this number zero for the first month, which she's done. Here's why: by starting at zero, it becomes incredibly easy for Lucy to see how much she's saved or overspent. The end balance is a number that's automatically calculated when Lucy adds her income and expenses. Starting at zero means that by month's end her savings is reflected in the end balance. A positive number indicates savings and a negative number indicates overspending (or not enough income). In Lucy's case, assuming she has no more transactions for the month, she was able to save $1,569.

Pro Tip: If you simply want to see how much you're saving each month, then make your starting balance $0 every time. It's much easier to trend your savings, and at the end of the year, you can add up each months' savings for your yearly total. In our example, Lucy is off to a good start!

Below the start and end balances, you'll see the comparison of Lucy's expenses to income. On the left, she has her expenses, and on the right, her income. Under the expenses column, she created the categories in which she spends most of her money. These are food, home, transportation, pet, utilities, phone, student loans, and extra spending. These don't have to be your exact groupings; you can choose anything you want, but they need to be mandatory expenses. In other words, they're things you *must* pay every month. For now, ignore the "extra spending" category. I'll talk about that in a little bit.

To the right of her categories is where Lucy entered her planned or estimated monthly expenses for each class she designated. The other two columns you see there, actual and difference, are left alone. As you'll soon see, when Lucy enters information in the Transactions tab, it will automatically populate these two columns.

On the opposite side of the page, the income section is set up in the exact same way. Lucy created her categories and entered her expected income. Again, the remaining information will automatically be filled from values inserted in the Transactions tab.

Now let's look at the Transactions tab where Lucy inserted *actual* income and expenses after they occurred:

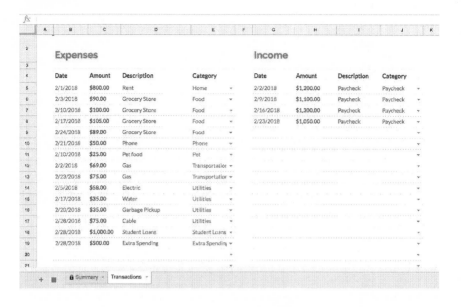

This tab is pretty easy to follow. Lucy simply listed the date and amount of her transaction. She typed a little description for more detail and chose the correlating category. She did the same for her income. These amounts are all automatically pulled over to the Summary tab where Lucy can then see the difference between her planned and actual spending. Google Sheets then calculated Lucy's actual expenses ($3,081) versus her actual income ($4,650), which is the end balance number we talked about at the beginning ($1,569). Remember, Lucy's end balance reflects how much she's saved this month. We've come full circle! Now, let's talk about creating *your* budget.

Your Budget

Setting up your monthly budget may seem somewhat time-consuming. It's true that creating your initial budget will involve a larger time commitment because you're starting from scratch. However, once you have your monthly template, you'll be able to reuse it for the following months, only making minor adjustments when needed.

To start, you'll need to predict your estimated monthly income and expenses just as Lucy did. Think back to last month as your reference. Try to make it as accurate as you can, but don't get overwhelmed and bogged down trying to remember every dollar spent. By doing this, you're creating your projected monthly budget.- The goal is to stick to or come in under this projected budget. Understandably, this may not be possible every month, but it should be a goal you strive to reach.

First, let's look at how to find the amount of your average paycheck. If you're salaried and your pay is always the same, then just skip to the next paragraph. Now, this may seem complex, but it's as simple as adding together your last few paychecks and dividing by the total number of checks. For example, if your past four pay stubs were $1,000, $1,500, $1,200, and $1,320, adding up to $5,020, then divide that by four, and your average paycheck is $1,255.

Now that you know the amount of your average paycheck, you need to find your average monthly pay. Consider the month for which you're budgeting and determine how many pay periods are in it. This is easy for people who are paid weekly. On the other hand, if you're paid every other week, you'll likely have two or three paydays. You'll multiply your average paycheck by the number of pay periods that month. Using our example from above, if you were paid twice during the month, your average monthly income would be $2,510. If you were paid three times, it would be $3,765. Now that you know your average monthly salary, you can input this number into your planned income section.

Next, we'll determine your estimated expenses. It is important to count only *mandatory* expenses you need for everyday life, as you saw in Lucy's budget. This is where you realize your Starbucks addiction isn't a mandatory expense. Examples of mandatory monthly expenses are things such as mortgage/rent, food, pet care, transportation, insurance, utilities, wireless bill, and student loans.

Once you determine your mandatory expenses, you need to estimate how much you spend per month in these categories. Some expenses, such as your mortgage/rent, student loans, and phone bill, are probably a set amount that's easy to input. However, items such as food, utilities, pet care, and transportation may vary from month to month. Therefore, to determine these expenses, you'll have to use the same approach we used when calculating your average monthly income. The easiest way of doing this would be to find bank or credit card transactions for these things and average your monthly spending on each.

Lastly, some things you might only pay once or twice a year, such as your car insurance or home insurance. For these expenses, find the total amount you pay and divide by 12 to break it down into monthly spending.

Now you can begin to list your mandatory expenses under the aptly named "expenses" section. To the right of each category, you'll place your newly calculated averages in the "planned" column.

Congratulations, you now have most of your projected monthly budget created! Before moving on, take a moment to look at your estimated monthly income and expenses. If your planned monthly expenses are greater than your planned monthly income, you have a problem. Think about that for a moment. If you've already planned on spending more than you make, you're going to find yourself in serious financial trouble in no time.

Since you were only supposed to list mandatory monthly expenses, you may be limited in where you can cut spending to fix this problem. However, if you've found yourself in this situation, you can try to lower your mandatory expenses by moving to find cheaper rent, getting a roommate, driving less and carpooling or walking more, shopping at a cheaper grocery store, or calling your utility or phone company and threatening to cancel your account if you don't get a better price. You may have to get resourceful in your solutions, but it's crucial to get your monthly planned expenses under your monthly planned income. If you've done all you can to lower your expenses, don't forget, you can try to increase your income as well. Getting a second job like driving for Uber or Lyft, shopping for Instacart, filling out online surveys, writing a book, or becoming a YouTube sensation may be an option. If you put your mind to it, you can find tons of ways to boost your income. Get creative!

Once your projected income is greater than your planned expenses, you're one step closer to financial independence. Subtracting your expenses from your income gives you your potential monthly savings. Multiply that number by 12 to get your *potential* savings for the year. Now that you see the amount of money you can save, it's time to determine a budgeting guideline to follow.

A lot of investment classes teach you the 50/30/20 rule. This rule states 50% of your yearly spending should go toward these mandatory expenses, 30% can go toward discretionary expenses, and 20% should be saved. However, I suggest more of a 50/20/30 or even a 50/10/40 rule. You're going to be hard-pressed for retirement and building a savings if you only save 20%. Therefore, the more you can save the better. You can create your own goal and always adjust it as you go. A budget doesn't have to be set in stone. It can grow and change as your life does.

To better understand, let's look at how Tyler uses the traditional 50/30/20 rule. Tyler makes $40,000 for the year after taxes. According to the rule, he should be spending around $20,000 on mandatory expenses, $12,000 on discretionary expenses, and saving $8,000 a year. While saving $8,000 for the year isn't bad, Tyler could be saving a lot more if he cut his discretionary spending down to 20%. If he used a 50/20/30 rule, Tyler would be saving $12,000! That's a big difference in savings while it still leaves $8,000 for discretionary spending!

Compare your budget to Tyler's. If your mandatory expenses are under 50% of your yearly income, good for you! However, if they're over 50%, try some of the previously mentioned strategies to save more and give you peace of mind.

Let's look at another example. You create your planned monthly budget, and you project your income to be $2,880 and your expenses to be $1,200. Therefore, you're projecting to spend approximately 40% of your income on mandatory expenses. With this information, and being the young, ambitious budgeter that you are, you decide to set a goal of 40/20/40. Remember, this means you would spend 40% ($1,200/month) of your income on mandatory expenses, 20% ($576/month) on whatever you so desire, and the remaining 40% toward your savings. That's a big-time savings goal!

The last thing you'll want to consider when creating your budget is your discretionary spending. These are all of your purchases that aren't mandatory but certainly add to your quality of life. These could be things like drinks with friends, a new outfit, your morning Starbucks fix, or travel. Whether you chose a 50/30/20 or 50/20/30 rule to guide you, don't forget to allot for this type of spending in your budget.

If you remember Lucy's budget, she had an "extra spending" category in her expenses. Budgeting isn't meant to force you to live a frugal life. It's done so you can see where you're spending money and where you can cut back in order to reach financial goals. Thus, some sacrifices will have to be made in order to reach those goals, but that's a part of everyday life. Better get used to it now!

Before ending this chapter, I want you to understand that just because you allot discretionary spending of 20% (or whichever percentage you chose) doesn't mean you're obligated to spend that amount. In the long run, the more you save now, the more opportunities you'll have to grow this money and build a better future for yourself! Of course, I'm not telling you to forego a once-in-a-lifetime vacation or experience; however, you need to be conscious of your spending and create goals to better your finances.

Long-term View

Some of you may read this section and say, "Alright, I can do this for a while, but I'm not going be able to budget forever." I feel you. I know it's not realistic for you to keep track of every dollar spent for the rest of your life. Some people are able to do this and enjoy doing it—that's fantastic. But for those of you who aren't excited by this process, I ask you to try it for six months to a year. If you really put forth an effort during this time, you'll be surprised by how easily budgeting becomes a healthy habit. After a few months, you'll gain a feel for how much extra money you can spend without counting dollar for dollar.

If you're still worried about your commitment to budgeting, I would suggest making it so simple that you have no excuse not to do it. Use an app or template on your phone, so it's easily accessible to you anywhere at any time. If you're not motivated enough to create the template or simply don't have the spare time, take advantage of apps that do the work for you, or feel free to email me at Brandon@strugglehood.com, and I'll create one for you. Yeah, that's how important I think this whole budgeting thing is. This is your financial life, and I'm willing to help you in any way I can. You'll truly be amazed at how easy it is to achieve your financial goals once you've started the budgeting process.

You now have all the knowledge and tools necessary to create your first budget. I hope I've shown you that everyone would benefit from a budget, no matter their financial situation. Most importantly, if you're living paycheck to paycheck, drowning in credit card debt, wondering where all your money has gone, or thinking you'll never be able to buy a home or even retire, then you need to start budgeting NOW. Our education system has failed us in teaching the value of budgeting. Consequently, most people don't attempt to take control of their finances until it's too late. Please don't be part of that crowd. Create a budget, set goals, track your spending, and when you're able to make a dream purchase or retire on time, you'll look back and be so happy you did.

Chapter 4:

Checking & Savings

With all of the extra money you're going to have from budgeting, you'll need somewhere to store it, which brings us to the concept of checking and savings accounts. The first account you open at a bank is usually a checking account. This is an account easily accessible by check (yes, they do still exist) or debit card. A checking account isn't traditionally used for large amounts of money because you earn little to no interest on the amount stored in the account. Therefore, you should only keep enough money in your checking account for a month's worth of everyday purchases and bills. Any more than that isn't doing you any favors. It won't grow and accrue any substantial interest. Even worse, if you lose your debit card or your PIN number is stolen, a thief has access to *all* of your hard-earned money. Don't let yourself end up in that position!

A checking account can be opened at a local bank, national bank, credit union, or even an online bank. Some institutions will offer benefits, such as free checks or even free money, for opening a checking account with their branch! So, shop around before opening your account. However, always pay close attention to the fine print because there may be a minimum deposit amount required to open the account and fees if it dips below that number. If you plan to travel frequently, it's probably worthwhile to open an account with a larger, national bank. This can save you from having to use foreign ATMs—as in not your bank's—and paying a fee to do so.

One last thing I want to mention about your checking account is an emergency fund or SOLF (shit outta luck fund). Let's face it; shit happens. We all know it; so, it's imperative that you have money set aside for just this instance. It could be car repairs, a sudden home repair, an illness or accident, or, if you live in Chicago like me, a mugging. Obviously, no one wants something like this to happen, and you certainly don't know when it'll happen. Your SOLF should be money put aside in your checking account that you'll never touch unless it's an emergency. I recommend using your checking account to avoid any potential withdrawal or transfer penalties associated with savings accounts. Most importantly, you'll have quick access to the money. I know, I know. You're saying, "Brandon, you just told me to keep only enough in my checking account for a month's worth of bills and everyday purchases. You're confusing me!" I did that for a reason. I want you to think of your checking account as exactly that: enough money for a month or so. I want the SOLF never to be thought of or touched until the need arises, and there will be a need eventually. If you can, put $800-$1,500 aside for your SOLF, and don't touch it. If that's too much money, don't sweat it. Start to build your SOLF as best you can while maintaining your set monthly amount in your checking account. **You should, however, reach your SOLF goal before moving on to opening any other accounts.**

Now you've got a solid checking account, and your SOLF is maxed out. That brings us to savings accounts. Savings accounts are used for larger amounts of money because they accrue interest on the money stored in them. The amount of interest is rather modest, averaging from 0.01%- 0.06%. Some people have a checking and savings account with the same bank. A perk to this is that you're able to link the accounts and transfer money between the two very easily. A savings account can be opened at the same time, or later than your checking account. Most savings accounts usually limit the number of withdraws you make, so it's traditionally not used for everyday spending.

Similar to how you fund your checking account, you should have a set amount you'd like to keep in your savings account. You should aim to keep about three to six months' worth of living expenses in your savings. I realize that doesn't just happen overnight. As with your SOLF, just start adding more and more in as you go. Remember, this will be easy to do once you realize how much money you're saving by budgeting your expenses.

Maybe you're like me and looked at those interest rates of 0.01%-0.06% and think, "That's it? That's practically nothing!" If so, you're right. That isn't much at all. Why not put your money in a savings account that actually will reward you for leaving your money in there? In order to get more bang for your buck, you can place your money in a high-yield savings account. Typically, online banks give you the highest interest rate because they don't have the costs of maintaining branches like traditional banks do. The average interest earned for these accounts is 1.30%- 1.60%.

Here's an example to help illustrate the difference. You've been budgeting away to build your savings to $10,000. For the sake of this example, we'll assume you're not making additional deposits into this account. In a traditional savings account earning you 0.01% interest, you would have $10,001 at the end of the year. On the other hand, if you put your $10,000 into a high-yield savings account earning 1.6% interest, you would have $10,160 at the end of the year. This is a difference of $160 in just one year; after ten years the difference would be $1,720.26.* Your savings would grow even larger if you continued to make monthly deposits into the account. You can see how this is more advantageous than storing your money in a traditional savings account.

I googled "best high-yield savings accounts," and it revealed multiple online accounts with great interest rates. At the time of writing, Barclays is offering 1.5%, Ally and American Express Savings are offering 1.45%, and Discover has a rate of 1.4%.[6] These are all just from a quick, five-second search. As you can see, it's not difficult to find high-yield savings accounts. Just research a few to see which one best suits your goals.

Another risk-averse way to save your money and earn interest is by opening a Certificate of Deposit (CD). CDs differ from savings accounts because you agree to put your money in this account and not access it for a set amount of time, or term. The average term length ranges from three months to six years. If you do withdraw the money early, you'll be subject to a penalty. Therefore, prior to opening a CD, you should be nearly certain that you wouldn't need this money in the foreseeable future. However, if you're willing to put the money away and not touch it, you can reap benefits. For example, a well-paying CD can pay anywhere from 1.80% interest on a one-year term and up to 2.55% interest for a six-year term. This six-year commitment would turn your $10,000 initial investment into $11,630.92, a difference of $631.69 from your high-yield saving account and a difference of $1,624.92 from your average savings account.[*]

All of these interest earnings are based on how the interest is compounded. I'll get more into compounding interest later in the book. For now, I will tell you that choosing an account that compounds interest daily or weekly is more advantageous than choosing an account that compounds interest monthly or yearly. More on this and savings in the retirement chapter!

Lastly, people may choose to invest their money in the stock market. The return on your investment usually is substantially larger than the savings accounts discussed above. However, with great reward comes great risk. For the purpose of this book, I will not dive further into the stock market. It could be a separate book in and of itself. That being said, I suggest a diversified savings profile that includes a mix of all of these accounts.

Pro Tip: If you want to get involved in the stock market, you can take advantage of robo-advisors such as Wealthfront or Betterment. A robo-advisor is an automated, online service that will automatically manage your portfolio. After indicating your risk tolerance, it will use a computer algorithm to make investments for you at fractions of the cost of a financial advisor.

I'd like to emphasize here that I'm not a financial professional, and these are only my opinions and recommendations. You should consult a professional before making any big financial decisions.

Okay, now that the legal jargon is out of the way, we can move on to the next chapter. You've learned how to create and organize your own budget and grow your savings account by leaps and bounds. This adulting thing isn't so bad, right? Good. In the next two chapters, you're going to learn about credit and debt, with which a lot of young people struggle. No one ever really taught us how we should properly balance the yin and yang of credit and debt, until now! It doesn't have to be all scary. As you read on, you'll see a smartly managed credit card can offer huge rewards.

Chapter 5:

Credit

My first introduction to credit came when I was a sophomore in college. I moved out of the dorms and found this tiny little apartment—albeit, right next to the dorms—that I would share with a roommate. We were men now, living on our own. The dorms were one thing, but this was it. We were fully functional adults. Gone were the days of eating cafeteria food, dealing with RAs, and signing in visiting guests. We could do whatever we wanted.

Since this was a college town and all this property did was rent to young college students, we had little trouble signing the lease. However, when I started to set up the utilities, the electric company wouldn't allow me to be the sole name on the account. They said I would need a co-signer because I basically had no credit history. Up until this point, I was completely unaware that you couldn't open utility accounts in your name without having some sort of established credit score. A phone call to my mom helped alleviate the issue, but I quickly got a reality check that I was nowhere near adulthood.

Maybe some of you have had similar experiences. Without any formal education on this topic, we're left to learn about building credit through life experiences such as my encounter with the electric company. No one cares how embarrassing it might be for us or how silly or foolish it may make us feel. That's not going to be you, though. You've already taken the initiative and gotten ahead by reading this book. My goal is to make it incredibly easy to understand the basics of credit and debt management. I want to answer important questions we've all found ourselves asking: What exactly is a credit score? How do I build credit or repair bad credit? What should I know about credit cards? How can I get out of debt safely? These next two chapters will explain all of that and much more.

What Is Credit?

Credit is the trust that allows a lender to provide something of value now to a borrower in which the borrower is contractually obligated to repay the lender later, usually with interest.[7]

Easy enough, right? The trust that's built is reflected in your credit score. Basically, your credit score is a numerical value that represents your "trustworthiness" or, in this case, "creditworthiness." The Fair Isaac Corporation created the type of credit score that we'll discuss in this book. You may have seen it referred to as a FICO score. For the purposes of this book, I'll use FICO score and credit score (rating) interchangeably. The scores range from 300 to 850. Higher scores reflect more trustworthy people in terms of their likelihood of paying back their debts promptly. Typical credit scoring usually looks something like this:

- >800: Excellent
- 700-799: Good
- 650-699: Fair
- 550-649: Poor
- <550: Bad

These ratings can vary, depending on whom or what institution you're trying to borrow from. Sometimes, a score of 750 would be considered excellent.

Your credit score represents your financial responsibility. Think of it as a grade for how well you're performing at personal finance. You're always being graded on something: job performance, driving record, your Uber rating, or how many likes or retweets you receive on social media. Get used to it. Entities such as banks, credit unions, credit card companies, or leasing offices can run a credit check to verify your credit. Your score can directly affect whether or not you qualify to receive a loan, get that new credit card, or even sign a new lease to that fancy high-rise apartment you found. Hopefully, you can see why this is so important to routinely monitor. Apps and websites such as *Credit Karma* make it very easy to keep track. Credit card companies, such as American Express, Capital One, and Discover, offer free ways to see your FICO score, whether it's on their app or on your monthly statement.

You may be wondering at this point, "Who makes these scores?" That's a great question. The United States has three major credit reporting agencies: Equifax, Transunion, and Experian (or The Big 3 as I like to refer to them). These three agencies, or credit bureaus, will use five factors when evaluating and generating a person's creditworthiness and credit score:

1. Payment history (this makes up 35% of your total credit score)
2. Amounts owed (30%)
3. Length of credit history (15%)
4. Credit mix (10%)
5. New credit (10%)

Payment History

Payment history is the most critical aspect in computing your FICO score. It makes up 35% of your overall score. Of the five factors contributing to your credit rating, payment history is the simplest to understand. Do you pay your bills on time? If not, how late are your payments? The later the payment, the more it affects your credit. The Big 3 also look at whether or not you've had any overdue bills going to a collection agency, foreclosures, bankruptcies, wage garnishes (a court order to deduct money from your earnings in order to pay off a debt), lawsuits, etc. Any of these incidents immediately let a credit agency know that you have difficulty paying off your debts and, therefore, aren't that financially reliable or, in their terms, creditworthy.

The frequency of missed payments is also a factor. However, as time wears on, missed payments become less of a negative influence. For example, let's say that six years ago, you missed a few credit card payments. Ever since then, you've made all your payments without trouble. Over the course of those six years, the negative impact of those missed payments lessens. It is also very important to note that late payments only stay on your credit history for seven years. Make it one more year with good payment history, and those missed payments will no longer affect your credit score.

When I graduated college, I was operating under the assumption that paying my bills on time was the only thing that went into building good credit. I had no idea what made up a credit score. I had a credit card that I basically *never* used. I would go months without ever using it. My thought process was this, "I have a credit card, but by not using it often, it shows I'm reliable and can pay for things without going into debt. I bet my credit score is through the roof!" Boy, did I have that wrong. I didn't have any payment history to prove I was reliable. Thirty-five percent of my credit score was reliant upon a factor that was practically nonexistent! You don't have to make that same mistake! #knowledgeispower #endthestrugglehood

Amounts Owed

The second most important factor in your credit score is amounts owed. This makes up 30% of your total score. Within the amounts owed category is a concept not many have heard of: credit utilization ratio (CUR). It carries significant weight in determining that 30%. CUR is a ratio that looks at how much debt you have versus your available credit limit.

Pretend you have two credit cards, each with a limit of $5,000 for a total of $10,000. Between those two cards, you have $2,500 of outstanding debt. This means your CUR is 25% (2,500/10,000 = 0.25). A CUR of 25% is good. I recommend trying to keep your ratio under 30-35%. Now, say you decide that two credit cards are too much for you, and you're afraid you might get into some spending trouble if you keep them both. You decide to cancel one of those credit cards. This causes your CUR to shoot up to 50% (2,500/5,000 = 0.5). This would negatively impact your credit score because it now looks like you're relying heavily on credit and appear to be more of a risk.

Pro Tip: You can call your credit card company and ask them to extend your credit limit. This would lower your credit utilization ratio, thus, bettering your FICO score. However, this shouldn't be considered an invite to charge more to your credit card and go further into debt!

Length of Credit History

The third factor contributing to your overall credit score is your length of credit history. This makes up 15% of the total score making it another important aspect to keep in mind. It's pretty self-explanatory. The Big 3 want to know how long you've used credit. In other words, how old are your accounts? The older the account is, the better it looks for you. Older accounts demonstrate reliability (assuming the account isn't littered with late payments). The overall average age of all your accounts will also contribute to your standing. Newer accounts bring down the overall average, therefore, lowering your score.

Because of this, it's not a good idea to close out your oldest credit card account. This is beneficial on two different fronts. First, having an open account will increase your CUR. Remember, the higher your credit limit, the better, as long as you don't continually spend up to that credit limit! Second, as we just discussed, your length of credit history contributes 15% to your overall credit rating. So, closing your oldest account can negatively impact your credit. It would be better for you to keep it open and not use it.

Remember the credit card I told you about that I never used? Yeah, so I got the card when I was in college (my first credit card!) through my bank at the time. However, after graduation, when I moved to a different state, I switched banks because that particular bank wasn't located there. Naturally, I closed all my accounts with my old bank, including the credit card. I thought that's just what one does. Thus, when I applied for a new credit card not long after, I was left wondering why my credit score was lower than I anticipated. I now had a very limited length of credit history.

New Credit

The next two factors each make up 10% of your FICO score. The first is new credit. When examining new credit, The Big 3 are looking at how many of your accounts are new and when was the last time you opened a new account. This should be taken into consideration if you want to boost your credit utilization ratio. It would be better to ask for an extension of your credit limit on your current card rather than open a new account simply for that purpose.

Newer accounts lower the overall average age of all your accounts and, in turn, lower your score. So not only should you keep from closing your older accounts, you should aim only to open new accounts if absolutely necessary.

Opening new accounts or even just applying for a line of credit, such as a loan, will result in something called a hard inquiry (hard credit check). Two types of credit checks exist: hard checks and soft checks. Hard credit checks become part of your actual credit history. They'll affect your overall score adversely. A soft credit check doesn't impact your credit rating. Soft checks are done when you check your credit yourself on something like *Credit Karma.* Or maybe a potential employer will run a background check that utilizes a soft credit check to determine if they think you're a responsible person. The take-home message here is that soft credit checks have no bearing on your credit score, but hard checks do. You should be fully aware every time a hard credit check is run, and make sure to limit those hard checks to once or twice a year if possible. Also, don't ever be afraid to ask the creditor if they plan to do a hard or soft credit check.

Credit Mix

The last 10% is made up of your credit mix. This is simply the different types of credit you have. Credit cards, mortgages, installment loans (a loan that's repaid in regular installments, such as a car payment) and specific store accounts (a Macy's card) are examples of a credit mix you potentially could have. Your total amount of accounts is also considered. Think of it like this: the more account types you have in good standing, the more it shows you're reliable enough to handle various credit types. However, I don't recommend opening random accounts just to increase your credit mix. It doesn't hold enough weight in your FICO score to do that.

Since I mentioned installment credit above, I'll touch on the difference between installment and revolving credit briefly. Very simply, installment debt is a loan in which you've agreed to pay back in routine installments. If you have a $300 monthly car payment, that's considered an installment loan. A credit card would be an example of revolving credit. Your credit limit remains the same despite the amount charged each month. For instance, let's say you owe $500 on your credit card statement this month and your credit limit is $5,000. You pay that bill in full (which you should *always* do monthly), but your credit limit remains the same. Because of your payment, you can again charge up to $5,000 the next month. This is revolving credit.

On a side note: if you don't pay your full balance every month, your credit limit wouldn't be $5,000. You must deduct the outstanding balance. In other words, if you only paid $250 instead of the full $500, then your remaining credit limit would be $4,750. Make sense?

How to Build (or Repair) Credit

Now that you know what credit actually is and what factors make up your overall score, let's talk a little bit about how to build good credit. Some of these points may have been alluded to in the previous section, but I feel they're important enough to drive home. Plus, it's nice to have them all here in one little section for times when you may want to come back and reread.

Starting out trying to build credit is a catch-22 situation. Lenders want to see an established track record of reliability, which is rather hard to prove when you're just setting out on your own with no credit history to speak of. Generally, you'll need about six months of credit activity being reported to The Big 3 before you're able to generate a FICO score of your own. Fortunately, a few opportunities are available to begin building your credit (or repairing if you've run into some trouble in the past).

One of the easiest things you can do is to become an authorized user on someone else's account. Maybe you have a parent, older sibling, or significant other who would add you to their credit card account as an authorized user. Obviously, you would want to make sure this person is reliable and has a good credit score. It won't do you any good to start building credit with someone who has thousands of dollars of credit card debt and a FICO score of 520. Being added as an authorized user allows you to use the credit card and build credit along the way without being reliable for the payments. Hopefully, you will have come to an agreement with the primary cardholder in terms of how you'll pay for whatever you charge to the card. This is a big opportunity to begin to build good credit. Don't be an ass by charging unnecessary things that you can't pay for and ruin yours and the primary cardholder's credit rating.

Another way to build credit is to have someone act a co-signer. Remember my story with the electric company when I was in college? I was fortunate enough that my mom was willing to be the co-signer on my utility bills until I could build up enough credit that she was no longer needed. You can have a co-signer for credit cards as well. This is basically someone with good credit vouching for you. It's important that the co-signer be fully aware that they're the ones on the hook for the full amount if you fail to make your payments. Again, don't be an ass. Hopefully, you can begin to see why having a good credit score credit score shows that you're responsible!

You can apply for something called a secured credit card account, in which you deposit cash up front. The amount deposited then works as your "credit limit." You're free to use the secured credit card just as you would a regular, unsecured credit card. For example, you'll have to make payments on or before the due date or interest will accrue on balances not paid in full. The difference here is that your cash deposit is used as collateral if you fail to make your payments. A secured credit card isn't meant for long-term use. It's meant to serve as a bridge. You can use it until you're able to qualify for an unsecured credit card. At that point, you'll be ready to enjoy the benefits of a real credit card (more on that later). Once you close the secured credit card, you'll receive your cash deposit back.

One final option I'll recommend in helping build your credit is to apply for a credit-builder loan. This is exactly as its name indicates. With a credit-builder loan, you can apply through a

Struggle

lender (bank or credit union) for a loan of smaller amounts ($500-$1,500). Once you're approved for the loan, the money is placed in an account to which you don't have access. You then must make the agreed-upon payments to the lender until the final payment is made. These payments could be as little as $100/month. Once the loan is paid in full, you get to keep the loan amount, and the lender will send a positive credit report to The Big 3. The credit-builder loan provides little risk for the lender. If, for any reason, you fail to make your payments, the agreement is void and the lender keeps the money. This little-known alternative can serve as an excellent starting block to building a strong credit score.

Once you've established a foundation and are on your own with good credit, it's extremely important to continue to make your payments on time. Remember, it counts for 35% of your overall FICO score. Keep making those payments, and keep watching that credit score climb!

Chapter 6:

Credit Cards and Debt Management

Now that you've built a good credit history, you're able to apply for a credit card. The benefits credit cards offer can be amazing if used properly. You just need to know what you're doing. Follow a few ground rules, and you can reap the many perks they have to offer!

Before getting into the types of benefits credit cards offer, you need to understand the fine line you're walking with a credit card. It's easy to get carried away and start charging all sorts of purchases to your card. After all, you swipe the card and go. You don't see any immediate deduction out of your bank account, making it seem like such an easy and hassle-free experience, which is exactly what they want you to think and feel. Keep in mind that at the end of the day, a credit card company is a business. They have various ways in which they make their money. One of those ways is relying on the fact that a *huge* percentage of cardholders don't pay off their bills in full every month. This is where a credit card's interest rate comes into effect.

Every time you use a credit card, you're borrowing money from that lender to cover that purchase, and you must pay to borrow that money. What you pay is the credit card's interest rate, which is also referred to as the annual percentage rate (APR). You can avoid paying any interest whatsoever if you pay your debt off in full every month when the statement closes. I'm going to repeat that because it's a monumentally important concept. **You can avoid paying any interest on purchases if you pay your balance off in full at the end of every billing cycle.** Read that again and commit it to memory. Write it down over and over 100 times if you must. Pay your balances off every month! Okay, I feel better now that I got that out.

Around the end of 2017, the national average APR was a little over 16%.[8] A lower credit score can cause this number to be even higher—another reason you want to stay on top of your credit score! APR is expressed as the interest you'll pay annually on your purchases. However, credit card companies use the APR to calculate interest over a monthly period. To break that down, just divide your APR by 365 (days in a year), and you'll get the daily percentage rate. So, if you had an APR of 16%, you could break that down to a daily rate of 0.0438% (16/365=0.043836).

Here's an example to help illustrate this concept and make it easier to follow. Let's say it's the beginning of the month and you go out and buy a new TV for $1,000 and charge it to your credit card. The card that you used has an APR of 16%. Assuming you've made no other purchases that day, an interest charge of 43 cents will be added to your total at day's end. You've read this book, so you know that you're going to have to pay that $1,000 off at the end of the statement period, so you make no other purchases with your credit card (strong work, I like it). The interest accumulates at 43 cents per day for the remainder of the month. That $1,000 purchase is now $1,012.90 (assuming 30 days in the month). However, credit card companies allow a grace period to pay your bill. So, if, at the end of the billing cycle, you pay off your full amount owed by the due date (sound familiar!?), you won't be charged that interest and will only have to pay $1,000. Always pay off your full amount every month!

If you don't make the full payment, the remaining balance is carried over into next month, and you'll see that interest charge appear on the next statement along with all the other charges you've made for the month. This can have a snowball effect rather quickly. The more purchases you make, the more interest you'll ultimately owe. It's incredibly easy to dig yourself into a hole and spend months or years trying to get out. All the while, your credit score is taking a hit.

Now you're aware of all the things that go into a credit score. You've built a strong credit foundation, and you're aware of the evils of APRs and how to avoid paying them. So, let's get you that credit card and start reaping the benefits!

Credit Card Benefits

As I mentioned before, various credit cards offer different kinds of perks. Credit card companies are always looking for ways to get new customers. In order to do so, they make some pretty worthwhile incentives. I could go on and on about the various benefits that are out there, but my aim here is to keep it simple and empower you with the basic knowledge to make the right decisions that suits your needs. I'll discuss three categories of benefits: cash back rewards, travel points, and low interest rates. These are simply some examples of cards that I'm familiar with, whether it be from personal experience or research.

Cash Back Rewards

If you've watched any sort of television in the last five years, you've probably seen a dozen commercials for credit cards that offer a "cash back" incentive. Credit card companies will do this in a number of ways. It can be a set percentage of your total purchase. The Citi Double Cash Card offers 2% back on all purchases. You get 1% back when you make the purchase and an additional 1% back when the purchase is paid off.

Some cards can offer a certain percentage back on specific types of transactions, such as grocery stores or gas stations. For example, I have the American Express Blue Cash Preferred Card. It offers 6% back at grocery stores; 3% back at all gas stations, department stores, and drug stores (CVS, Walgreens); and 1% back on all other purchases.

Or it could be a rotating perk every few months. The Discover It Card offers 5% back on all purchases made within a designated category. The category usually changes every four months. For example, at the time of writing, Discover was offering 5% back on all purchases made at grocery stores. Next month, it will change to restaurants.

It is important to keep in mind that no matter how great these offers sound, they still have high interests affixed to them. Cash back reward cards will usually have a higher interest rate. If you haven't already figured it out, I must continue to stress how important it is to use your credit card wisely while making sure to pay it off in full at the end each statement.

Travel Points

Instead of cash back, some credit card companies will offer travel points on made purchases. Some cards offer up to 50,000 free travel points if you use it to spend a few thousand dollars and pay it off. You can get credit cards through specific airlines, or you can use cards like the Capital One Venture Card. I prefer the Capital One Venture card because it can be used on all airlines with no restrictions. The Venture card offers double miles on every purchase. You can then convert those miles to help lower the cost of a flight or, if you have enough miles, fly for free! If you sign up for a specific airline's card, you're restricted to flying only on that carrier. This may not always work out depending on the price and times of their offered flights. I find it easier, knowing I can use my points on any airline.

Just as you can go through a specific airline, you can also get credit cards through specific hotels. A card like the Starwood Preferred Guest by American Express is a good example. This card offers double points for every dollar spent at a Starwood (think Sheraton or Westin) or-Marriot property and one point for every other purchase. These points can then be converted into discounted or free stays at their hotels throughout the world!

Low Interest Rates

Some companies will use a different approach to make themselves more appealing. Rather than offer cash back bonuses or travel points, some credit cards will offer 0% APR. Usually, this offer will only last for a promotional period such as eighteen months. The Chase Freedom Card offers 0% APR for fifteen months. It is important to note that once these promotional periods expire, the normal interest rates resume, which average around 16%.

A couple things worth mentioning are variable interest rates and annual fees. Most credit cards have variable interest rates meaning your interest rate can theoretically go up or down over time. Credit card companies will provide you with a range where you might expect your interest rate to land. If, for whatever reason, you can't pay off your balance at the end of the month, make sure to keep an eye on your interest rate, so you'll know what amount of interest is accruing.

The other item I want to mention is annual fees. Some companies will require an annual fee to use their card (just one more way for them to make money). Typically, cards that require annual fees offer larger rewards. For example, the Chase Sapphire Reserve credit card has an annual fee of $450. However, you earn three times the points per dollar spent on travel and dining while earning one point per dollar on all other purchases. Included with this card is a $300 travel credit and reimbursement for Global Entry or TSA PreCheck. Pretty nice perks!

On the other hand, many cards don't charge an annual fee. An example is the Bank of America Travel Rewards Credit Card. It offers 1.5 points for every dollar spent and no foreign transaction fees. Additionally, if you spend $1,000 in the first three months, you'll get an extra 20,000 points—equal to a $200 statement credit. These are still great perks for not having to pay a fee.

So, what should you do? If you're just starting out, I recommend a no fee card. Take a look at this scenario. Let's say you're approved for a new card with great travel rewards and an annual fee. A year later you haven't traveled much and decide you can't justify paying the fee. So, you close the account lowering your CUR and overall age of your accounts, ultimately dropping your credit score. However, if the card didn't have a fee, you simply could keep it open and not risk hurting your credit score. Therefore, I recommend annual fee cards for people with an excellent credit rating and those who have done a great deal of research into the risks/benefits of these cards.

Pro Tip: If the perks of the card best fit your needs, don't let an annual fee be your only deterrent. For example, a cash back rewards card will often cover the cost of the fee. Whereas the benefits of a travel rewards card will usually outweigh the cost of the fee (i.e., covering the cost of a flight).

At the end of the day, you want to choose the card that best suits you. Obviously, if you don't travel much or hate flying, then you should avoid getting a card that offers points for airline or hotel purchases. However, cash back rewards are a good option for almost everyone. Most companies allow you to use your cash back directly towards your monthly balance, which I think is a great option!

My last piece of advice regarding credit cards details how you should actually use them. We've talked about the importance of paying them off monthly. I'm sure you're as sick of reading it as I am of typing it. Good, I've made my point! However, I haven't really touched on how to use a credit card responsibly. Initially, you only need to open one card. Use that card the same as you would a debit card. Pay with a credit card on purchases you would normally be making anyway (groceries, gas). If you don't have the money to pay cash that day for whatever you're purchasing, you don't need to be buying it. You can't afford it. It's that simple. For example, if you're looking to buy a new computer for $800 and you can't pay for that new computer with a debit card, check, or cash right there on the spot, then you shouldn't be putting it on your credit card. This is where most people go wrong. Stick with this thought process, and you'll find yourself avoiding significant credit card debt.

With that being said...

How Should I Manage My Debt?

At some point, you'll inevitably find yourself wondering which debt you should be focusing on the most. You may have credit card debt, student loans, car payments, a mortgage, etc. Debt is emotionally exhausting! It's a constant stressor that's always on the back of your mind, whether you realize it or not. If you have any sort of outstanding debt, you're not financially free. Sometimes, that can feel overwhelming. Fear not! I'm here to help you manage that debt and fight your way to financial freedom!

Let's look at our pal Tammy to see how she manages her debt. Tammy has $4,000 in credit card debt with a 16% interest rate. Her minimum monthly payment would be roughly $140. She borrowed $72,000 in student loans at an interest rate of 6%, which has resulted in a monthly payment of $800. Tammy's car loan was for $21,700 at a 4% interest rate making her payment $200 per month. Of course, Tammy must make the minimum payments on all three of these debts. This would already be factored into her budget under the mandatory expenses category. However, Tammy has some extra cash this month and smartly wants to throw it towards her debt. She knows that she can make extra payments on her loans or credit card debt at any point. Naturally, she wants to put it towards her student loans because it's the highest principal balance; however, that wouldn't be the right move in this situation. Tammy should do whatever she can to pay off the debt with the highest interest rate—in this case, her credit card debt with the 16% APR. Paying off the debt with the highest interest rate first will save Tammy a lot of money over the lifetime of her loans. **Paying off your debts with the highest interest rates first (not the largest balances), is the best way to manage your debt.** If you're able to make additional payments like Tammy, then use the extra cash for your higher interest rate items first while continuing to make the minimum payment on all other debts.

Following my simple guidelines to manage your debt wisely will help you continue to build great credit. Also, it will allow you to receive low interest rates on mortgages or home equity loans should that time come. It's inevitable that most of us will take on some sort of debt. Great credit isn't built overnight. So, it's important to understand how to properly manage your debt.

I hope you were able to learn a few things about credit and debt. We often don't get the proper education necessary to understand what it means to be financially responsible. I hope I was able to enlighten you about credit cards and what all the fuss is about. And if you were anything like me, maybe you've realized that certain cards can actually be your friends!

Chapter 7:

Student Loans

What a great feeling it is to graduate. You're finally free! No more classes, tests, papers, projects, or late nights spent studying. You're ready for that new job it took months of applications and interviews to land. You go out and get new clothes for work, move into a new apartment, and get settled in a new city. You start your new job. The people are great, and you make new friends. Then the paychecks start rolling in. You've never had this kind of money before. Life is awesome! It was worth all those years spent studying and cramming.

Fast-forward six months to when you get a notification informing you that your student loan grace period is ending. "Oh shit! How did I forget about that?" The thoughts begin to race through your head:

> *How much are my payments? How do I make payments? Did I budget for this? What's my interest rate? I have multiple loans—how do I keep track of them all? What happens if I can't make a payment? Can I lower my payments?*

A lot of you have probably had a similar experience. After school, it's hard enough to get your feet under you and start functioning as a real adult. Getting the student loan bomb dropped on you just as you settle in can set you back. The cost of education these days is astronomical. It's a tough situation most of us are saddled with soon after graduating. I want to make it easy to start paying off your loans and give you confidence that you can get them paid off as soon as possible! It doesn't have to be such a big stressor. This part of the book will break down student loans and simplify what they are, how to pay them off, how to reduce the amount of interest, and how to consolidate and refinance your loans.

What Are Student Loans?

A student loan is a type of loan that's used to help pay for college and graduate school. It can be used to help cover the costs of tuition, books, supplies, housing, and costs of living. You apply for a student loan by completing a Free Application for Federal Student Aid (FAFSA). You then receive a letter from your school explaining the different options you have. Getting into the details of how to fully apply for a loan is for another time. I'm going to assume you've already completed that process. Once you qualify for a student loan, you should be aware of the types of student loans available: Stafford Loans (also referred to as Direct Subsidized Loans or Direct Unsubsidized Loans), Direct PLUS loans, and Perkins Loans.

A Direct Subsidized Loan is a type of loan that's generally given to students who are able to demonstrate financial hardship. Most of those awarded this type of loan come from families making less than $50,000/year. With this type of loan, you're not responsible for making any payments while in school, *and* the government will pay your interest during this time.

A Direct Unsubsidized Loan is one in which all students are eligible. Payments on these loans are usually postponed, or deferred, until after graduation. However, you're responsible for paying all interest that accrues over the lifetime of this loan, including while you're in school.

A Direct PLUS Loan can be broken down further into two categories: Parent PLUS Loan and Grad PLUS Loan. Both are relatively self-explanatory. A Parent PLUS Loan is for parents of a dependent child attending an undergraduate program. For students attending a graduate program, you can apply for a Grad PLUS Loan. Both of these loan types have no maximum amount and generally have a higher interest rate than the more traditional student loans mentioned above.

Perkins Loans are given to those who are able to demonstrate an exceptional financial need. They're a form of a subsidized loan given by the government. They have fixed interest rates of 5% and longer grace periods (nine months) than the Stafford loans (six months) with built-in special forgiveness provisions. Perkins loans were brought to an end as of September 30, 2017 [9] so they'll no longer be given out. However, I thought they deserved mention for the people who qualified and received them prior to their termination.

I'll briefly mention that you can apply for private loans that aren't granted by the federal government. They typically have higher interest rates and aren't built to suit the student necessarily. I recommend exhausting all of your options through the government before trying to secure a private loan for education.

The amount of loan you qualify to receive is based on a number of things. Considerations such as your family's expected contribution towards your tuition, the cost of attending your school, your year in school, and whether or not you're a full or part-time student are all influential. It needs to be noted that just because you qualify for a certain loan amount doesn't mean that you have to accept the entire amount. My advice is to take the absolute minimal amount you need to get through the semester. Trust me; it will save you a lot of money down the road.

Fall from Grace

As I've alluded to earlier, your loans are typically placed in deferment while you remain at or above half-time student status. This simply means you're not required to make any payments on your loan at this time, but interest is still accruing. After graduation, you're typically afforded a grace period (six months) until you have to begin the repayment process. The grace period allows you enough time to find a job, potentially relocate, start generating income, and hopefully, decide on a repayment plan. If, prior to the end of your grace period, you enroll back into school at half-time status or greater, or you're called to active military duty, your grace period will reset once you get out of school or the service.

Pro Tip: It's important to know that Direct PLUS Loans don't have a grace period. So, your repayment will begin immediately upon graduation.

Even though you aren't making any payments during this six-month window, interest will still accrue on most loans. However, I'll let you in on a little-known secret. You're able to make payments on your interest while in school. This affords you a couple of benefits. First, it saves you money by reducing your overall payment once you're out of school. I'll spare you the math behind it, but it could save you hundreds of dollars! It doesn't lower your principal balance, but by having some of the accrued interest already paid off, it will ultimately save you a bundle in the end. The second benefit from paying off interest while in school is that you would develop a habit of paying your loans in a timely fashion. A habit of making a monthly interest payment will cause you to be less likely to forget or miss your first payment when the grace period ends.

Now that you have a better understanding of the type of loan(s) you could have, let's look at how to actually begin to repay those loans once the grace period ends.

Chapter 8:

Paying Back Your Loans

The time has come. That carefree, six-month window is ending, and you've got to start paying back the mountain of student loan debt you've accumulated. This type of debt is the proverbial monkey on your back for millions of people. I want to simplify the process for you and get you monkey-free as soon as possible!

You can choose from among eight options to begin paying back your loans. I recommend speaking directly to your loan servicer or checking out their website to get a full understanding of your options. You can also google "student loan payment calculator," enter some of your information, and see your estimated monthly payments. Since you have eight options when deciding how to repay your loans, the task can be more complicated than just making a simple monthly payment. **The most important concept I want you to understand from this chapter is that the longer it takes to repay your loans and/or the lower your monthly payments are, the more money you'll pay over the lifetime of the loan.** This is due to interest. We'll discuss interest and why it's public enemy #1 shortly.

The default payment option is the Standard Repayment Plan. Under this plan, all borrowers are eligible. You'll make a fixed, monthly payment for up to 10 years before your loan is paid in full. You can work directly with your servicer to make larger, fixed payments in order to have your loan paid off in under 10 years.

The Graduated Repayment Plan is also available to all borrowers. With this plan, your payments will start lower and increase (graduate) every two years. You can also choose to pay on this plan for up to 10 years. However, because your initial payments are lower, you'll ultimately pay more money over time. Again, this is due to interest.

Then there is the Extended Repayment Plan. To qualify, you must have more than $30,000 in outstanding loans. Payments under this plan can be fixed or graduated. Your payments will be lower than the previously mentioned plans, but it will take up to 25 years to repay your loans under this method.[10] Therefore, you'll pay even more with this plan than with the Standard or Graduated Plans.

The next group of repayment plans is based on your income. These plans have numerous eligibility requirements and stipulations. The details are too lengthy for this book. I'll just keep it simple and say that all of these plans will require you to pay *more* over time compared to the standard plan. That doesn't mean they're bad options. One of these plans may be all that you can afford, and that's perfectly fine. I just want you to be aware that they force you to pay more than the standard plan. The names of these plans are the Income-Based Repayment (IBR), The Pay as You Earn (PAYE), The Revised Pay as You Earn (REPAYE), Income-Contingent Repayment (ICR), and Income-Sensitive Repayment plans. For a detailed comparison of these plans, visit studentaid.ed.gov/sa/repay-loans/understand/plans.

Conflict *with* Interest

No matter the repayment plan and options you choose, one thing is inevitable: interest. Interest will be factored into all of your payments. It's the worst. Looking at the length of time it takes to repay your loans and the amount of interest that you'll end up paying is enough to make you sick. I'm getting fired up just thinking about it!

To illustrate the insane amount you can pay in interest, let's look at the following example: Meet Dan. Over Dan's collegiate career, he managed to borrow $50,000 in federal loans. He graduated in 4 years with a great degree and bright future. When his grace period ended, he selected the Standard Repayment Plan to repay the $50,000 over 10 years. His interest rate was 6% with a minimum monthly payment of $555. Dan proceeded to make the minimum payment for 10 years without issue. Great job Dan, right? Not quite. Upon closer examination, he discovered he paid $16,612 in interest alone! Dan's $50,000 loan actually cost him $66,612. Yep, that's right. Dan got worked on this deal. Don't be Dan.

This example is all too real for millions of Americans. So many begin paying back their loans when the grace period ends and never give it much thought—other than to make sure they don't miss a payment. Years go by, and they begin to wonder why their balance doesn't seem to be going away. The answer? Interest, of course.

So how do you avoid being like our buddy Dan? The first thing you can do is make additional payments when possible. Just because you have a 10 or 25-year term on your repayment schedule doesn't mean you actually have to use all of the allotted time. **There's *no penalty* for paying off your student loans early.** I repeat, no penalty. By making extra monthly payments, the principal balance on your loan is reduced. This means less interest will accrue over time and ultimately save you a lot of money. If you're paying on more than one loan and you're not sure which loan to make the extra payment, choose the loan with the highest interest rate. As I said before, paying off the loans with the higher interest rates will save you the most money over time. I realize not everyone has excess money lying around to throw at their loans. As you'll see in the next section, another potential option is available to save you money.

Loan Consolidation

Loan repayments can be confusing and messy. It's possible to have multiple loan payments with different due dates leaving you scrambling to figure out what's due when. Good news! You can consolidate your loans. Two types of student loan consolidations exist: private and federal. Private consolidation is sometimes referred to as refinancing. Refinancing is done through a private lender in order to get a lower interest rate. Your loans are also consolidated with the private lender. Federal student loan consolidation is done through the Department of Education (DOE) to help manage multiple loans. Confused yet? Let's examine what it means to choose one over the other.

Federal student loan consolidation is when all of your federal loans are combined into one—called a direct consolidation loan. This is a way to simplify your payments. You no longer need to worry about making all the individual payments or missing one and defaulting. Direct consolidation loans are sometimes done in order to qualify for an income-driven repayment plan.

A direct consolidation loan has a few disadvantages, however. By doing so, your interest rate won't be lowered. In fact, it often will increase. When you consolidate, your new interest rate is a fixed rate derived from a weighted average of all of your previous rates. It's then rounded to the nearest 1/8th percent. This will lead to you paying more in interest over the life of the loan. Depending on your type of loan, you could also lose access to some of the repayment options or forgiveness programs.[11]

Private loan consolidation can be used to combine federal, private, or a combination of both types of student loans. Refinancing into this type of loan is done by a private lender such as Sofi, Earnest, Laurel Road, or DRB (Darien Rowayton Bank). Ideally, with the new private loan, you'll be able to qualify for a lower interest rate, assuming you have a good credit history. Now do you see why I spent so much time trying to hammer that home? I'm only looking out for you!

Other factors that may be considered in determining your new interest rate are education, job history, and debt-to-income ratio. Even if you have a good credit score, having a lot of additional debt, will make it tougher to get a better interest rate from a private lender. Remember, it all boils down to the type of risk, or creditworthiness, you present.

When searching for a private lender, you can provide them with some basic information about you and your loan amounts. In return, they'll offer you an *estimated* range of potential interest rates. This range is generally rather broad, but a higher credit score will usually keep you near the lower end of the range. Your rate will also depend on whether or not you choose fixed or variable interest.

Fixed interest rates stay the same throughout the life of the loan; whereas, variable rates fluctuate with the financial market. Initially, variable rates will often be lower than fixed. This is because you're assuming a risk by selecting a variable rate, so lenders will reward that risk with a lower rate. You should be aware, however, that, at any point, a variable rate could increase and ultimately become higher than the fixed rate. Let's look at some pros and cons of each type.

A fixed interest rate is a better option for those who are less risk-averse. Always knowing what your monthly payment will be is a luxury some love having. A fixed rate is better for someone paying over a longer period of time because your rate remains constant. As you know, a variable rate will fluctuate with the economy. Therefore, over the course of a lengthy loan repayment, the chances of your variable rate going up are higher. The higher your variable rate climbs, the more interest you end up paying over the lifetime of the loan. However, if interest rates don't increase, there's a chance the fixed rate will actually have you paying more interest than the variable.

Conversely, a variable interest rate is a good choice for someone who plans to repay their loan in a short time frame. If you know you'll be able to afford extra payments, then a variable rate is a good option because of the initial lower rate. Or maybe you just want lower payments initially but will be able to make higher payments in a few years. Think of it in terms of going from an entry-level salary to making more money as your career progresses. Maybe you just like taking chances. If you think the market will remain low, then choosing a variable rate could be the right decision for you. Ultimately, it's an important decision that only you can make. Use this advice to figure out where you stand, and weigh all of your options.

Once you've determined which type of rate you want, you'll actually have to apply through the lender. During this process, the lender will run a hard credit check. Recall that a hard check will become part of your credit history temporarily lowering your score. It's important to keep this in mind if you decide you want to compare lenders to see the best rate. Generally, if this is all done within a 30-day window, it will all be considered as one inquiry. Once the hard credit check is completed, the private lender will give you the *actual* interest rate you'll pay if you choose to refinance. If you accept the offer, the private lender pays back the issuers of your loans the full amounts, shouldering all of your student loan debt. You'll then begin making one monthly payment to your private lender with the new interest rate factored in.

Pro Tip: If you want an easy way to compare lenders without the hard credit check, look at NerdWallet's customizable comparison. You can find it at www.nerdwallet.com/refinancing-student-loans.

If you're unable to qualify for refinancing with a private lender, don't be discouraged. You can still consolidate your federal loans if you think it will benefit you to have one payment, but remember, it may increase your interest rate. Continue to build your credit using some of the strategies we've discussed. And when you're ready, reapply!

There you have it. You're on your way to successfully consolidating and/or refinancing your student loans. Congratulations!

Loan Forgiveness

I would be doing you a disservice if I didn't tell you a little bit about loan forgiveness programs. Several student loan forgiveness programs have very extensive qualifications. I want to make you aware that they exist and that you can possibly have some of your debt paid off by the government. I'll discuss two of the more popular forgiveness plans and provide you with options to obtain more information should you so choose.

Public Service Loan Forgiveness (PSLF) is for those with federal student loans who are employed full-time by a federal, state, or local government entity or nonprofit organization that the IRS designates as tax-exempt. If you work for a nonprofit that offers specific public services, you may also qualify. Examples of these types of work include military service, emergency management, public safety or law enforcement, public health services, public education, public library services, school library and other school-based services, early childhood education, or public interest law services.[12]

Once enrolled, you'll be able to receive full loan forgiveness after 120 qualifying payments are made. That equates to 10 years. This program was designed to keep people in lower paying public jobs—think social work—and reward them for their service by forgiving the remainder of their loan. My only issue with this is that after 10 years of payments, you could potentially have your entire loan already paid off! Unless you absolutely love what you're doing, most people will find it difficult to commit to a job for 10 years right out of school. I would recommend carefully examining your loans and determining where your loan balance will be in 10 years. If you plan to have them paid off or are very close to having them paid off, you'll want to consider whether or not it's worth the long commitment. I want you to understand that I'm not advising against this option. Rather, I want you to be able to see the full picture and not just see "loan forgiveness" and jump in with both feet. If you would like further information on this program, www.studentdebtrelief.us/forgiveness/public-service-loan-forgiveness is a great source to check out.

Teacher Student Loan Forgiveness (TSLF) is the other plan I'll briefly mention. With this program, teachers with five consecutive years of service teaching in low-income elementary or secondary schools will have their loans forgiven up to $17,500. To me, this is a little more reasonable than the 10-year requirement for the PSLF. If you're interested in learning more about TSLF, you can check out studentaid.ed.gov/sa/repay-loans/forgiveness-cancellation/teacher.

What if I Can't Pay My Loans?

Unfortunately, life can have its ups and downs. Unforeseen things sometimes happen, which leave you strapped for cash. Whether you lose your job because the economy takes a hit, you or someone in your family becomes ill, or your furnace ceases to produce heat in the dead of winter, you may find yourself asking, "What happens if I can't make my loan payments?"

I'll first tell you what happens if you miss your payments. Afterward, we'll look at all the options you can pursue in order to prevent from getting into that situation in the first place. It takes 270 days of missed payments for your federal loan to go into default. Private lenders' policies will vary, so make sure you know their terms and conditions if you have a private loan. Once your loan is in default, you'll face numerous negative consequences.

Defaulting on your loans can cause the entire balance of your loan, including interest, to become due immediately. The notice of default becomes part of your credit history and will negatively impact your score. Once you're in default on your loans, you can no longer receive deferment or forbearance (which we'll talk about shortly).

If in default, the government can garnish your wages, federal tax refunds, Social Security check, or your disability benefits, while a private lender really only has the option to sue. The government doesn't often sue because of these other ways it can collect money from you; however, when it does, it usually wins. If this happens, the government can place a lien on your home or even force a sale.[13] They'll get ya every time!

As you can see, this is a big deal and a situation in which you don't want to find yourself. Therefore, let's look at some things you can do before getting to this point. The first option you have if you feel you're unable to make payments is to contact your loan servicer. Keep in mind that the government or private lender provides student loans to make money. If you default on your loan and can't pay, they lose money. So, it's in their best interest to help you in any way possible. You and your lender should discuss any repayment plans that will be beneficial, such as an income-driven payment plan. It's also possible to have a portion of your paycheck deducted to help make your payments.[14]

A couple additional alternatives you have are to cut some expenses and/or increase your income by taking a second job or starting a side hustle. In the next chapter, I explain passive income and how you can use that to boost your current income. Taking a second job will inadvertently cause you to cut your expenses because you'll have less time to spend money on things. I know that doesn't sound glamorous, but it's better than defaulting on your loans. Hey, sometimes you gotta do what you gotta do.

Another option, if you haven't done so already, is to use this knowledge to refinance your student loans. Hopefully, this will provide you with a new, lower interest rate and ultimately a lower payment. On the flip side, if your problem isn't due to lack of funds but you simply missed payments because you have so many, try consolidating your loans into one.

If you've exhausted all of these other options, you can try to place your student loans in deferment or forbearance. While these aren't great options, they're definitely better than defaulting. Placing your loans in deferment or forbearance means you won't have to make payments for a set period. While in deferment, your loans will continue to accrue interest unless you have a subsidized loan. Deferment requires strict criteria to be met, and you must file the appropriate paperwork. To meet those criteria, you must be:

- Enrolled in school at least half-time
- Enrolled in a graduate fellowship program
- In an approved rehabilitation program for the disabled
- Unemployed and seeking employment
- Suffering economic hardship
- Serving in the Peace Corps
- Serving on active duty in the military [15]

Deferment is very beneficial to those with Direct Subsidized Loans since it's not accruing interest. With forbearance, on the other hand, you're also excused from making payments on your loans for a specified time. However, interest will accrue on all types of loans while in forbearance, which you'll be responsible for paying. As you can see, the main difference between deferment and forbearance is whether or not you'll have to pay the interest that accrues. Qualifying for forbearance is at the discretion of your loan provider and can usually be requested verbally. Generally, you're able to place your loans in forbearance if you show:

- Financial difficulties
- Medical expenses
- Change in employment
- Other reasons acceptable to your loan servicer

Something called mandatory forbearance is also available. You'll be able to qualify for this if:

- Your monthly payments are greater than 20% of your total gross monthly income
- You're in a medical or dental internship or residency program
- You're serving in AmeriCorps for which you received a national service award
- You're an activated member of the National Guard
- You're performing teacher service that would qualify you for teacher loan forgiveness [15]

If you're unable to meet the eligibility requirements for a deferment, you have a better chance of placing your loans in forbearance. Keep in mind that it is generally not possible to place your loans in either deferment or forbearance if your loans are already in default.

You can take many routes before defaulting on your loans. There's no right or wrong way to do it. Whichever of the above options best suits you, do it. Just do me a favor and **please don't pay your student loan debt with a credit card**! I understand that your student loan balance is such a large sum that you want to pay it off in any way possible. It's overwhelming to think of how much you have to pay back. Trust me; I've been there. However, using your credit card isn't the answer. Your student loans have an interest rate of somewhere around 7%, lower if you've refinanced! Your credit card's interest rate can be as high as double or triple your student loan's interest rate. So, if you transfer your payment from a 7% interest rate to a card that will now accrue 16% interest, that's not going to end well. Also, don't forget about the credit utilization ratio (CUR) we discussed. Your credit rating could take a hit if you add your student loan balance to your credit card because you'll likely be over that 30% threshold. If you need to, reread the credit and debt section about managing debt. Bottom line: find another way to pay your student loan debt, please.

Many of us have some sort of student loan debt. This chapter was meant to help you better understand those loans and guide you in how to plan and manage your payments properly. Use every resource you can. Check to see if you qualify for any forgiveness programs. If you can afford extra payments, make them! Refinance and lower those interest rates. Talk with your lender if you're having trouble. They'll do their best to help you; otherwise, they don't get paid. Consider all of your options if you're having trouble making payments: get a second job, cut expenses, find a roommate, and, if you must, request a deferment or forbearance. Use the advice in this book and you'll get those loans paid off in no time. I know it!

Chapter 9:
Retirement Planning

For a lot of us, retirement is a topic that doesn't capture our attention until it's often right around the corner. When I graduated and got those first paychecks, I felt like I was king of the world. I had money to go out on the weekends, to travel and see my friends, and to buy myself something every now and then. Life was good. Retirement planning was literally the furthest thing from my mind. I honestly don't know if I thought about retirement once while in my 20s except for skipping over it when filling out paperwork for a new job. The importance of planning early for retirement was never made clear to me. I hope to change that for you.

"Retirement? That's for people my parent's age!" This exact thought went through my mind as I was filling out paperwork for my first job out of school. I thought, "There's no need to contribute money to a retirement account. I've got plenty of time for that down the road. I want my paycheck as fat as possible, baby!" Looking back, it's actually quite funny how naive I was. But that's the problem! We're not presented an appropriate opportunity to learn these things when we should—while we're young. If you're in high school or college and reading this book (thank you btw), I seriously envy you. I mean it. You're putting yourself way ahead of the game. You're going to do big things!

It's clear I was missing some great opportunities to contribute to my retirement. My moment of realization happened when I was sitting in Chicago at my orientation for a new job. An HR representative was there. All the while, he kept harping on how great the benefits at this company were. He said things like, "We match 100% of your contribution to your 401(k) up to 6%, and you're vested after only one year!" People around me seemed pretty excited as they clapped and whistled. I was clapping, but I didn't know what in the hell he just said. It may as well have been another language. That did it. Just like so many other financial situations, I was tired of feeling so dumb. I decided right then and there that I was going to read and teach myself everything I could about retirement.

As with the other subjects in this book, it's my goal to make retirement planning as simple to understand as possible. I want to introduce you to the different types of retirement accounts and how they can work for you, compounding interest, ways to save as much as possible for retirement, and when you can actually retire. I also want to address any concerns you may have concerning social security and the direction it's headed.

Why You Should Care About Retirement Now

Just the other day, as I was listening to the radio while driving, a commercial popped on claiming that the median amount of money put away for retirement by the average American is only $5,000! I almost puked. I couldn't believe what I just heard. Take a minute to let that sink in. Five. Thousand. Dollars. Pretend for a minute this is you (we all know you're smarter than that, so we have to pretend). What do you think you could accomplish with that? You could never actually retire with that amount of money. So, plan on working until you die. Also, if you actually did retire, you'd be out of money in less than six months. I'm sure some of you just read that and thought to yourself, "I could make $5,000 last longer than that." If so, I'm glad you're reading this book! This chapter is definitely for you!

A common misconception is that Social Security will provide for a comfortable lifestyle in retirement, and a lot of people tend to get the mindset that Social Security is all they'll need. The average amount of money a retired person received in Social Security this past year was just over $1,400 per month.[16] That averages out to about $350 per week. You aren't going to be able to enjoy your golden years effectively on $350 a week! You must have other sources of income to continue to live the way you've become accustomed to living. No one wants to retire to a life of poverty!

Not contributing to retirement as early as possible will make it increasingly difficult to retire at the age you would like. Starting early allows you to take advantage of a concept called *compounding interest*.

As we discussed in Chapter 4, your savings account earns interest over time. Retirement accounts also earn interest. These accounts will grow at a much higher interest rate than a savings account would. When you open a retirement account, you'll accrue interest on your initial investment, say 5%. Therefore, after the first year, your investment has grown by 5%. However, after another year or two, you've not only earned interest on your investment but on the interest as well. In other words, your interest earned interest. It's rumored that Albert Einstein referred to compounding interest as the most powerful force in the universe! I don't know if he actually said it or not, but it doesn't matter. The fact that it's even debated draws enough attention to it that it should be examined more closely.

Let's use an example. Say you read this book when you were about to graduate high school and decided to put $500 from graduation gifts and savings from your job into a retirement account. You know starting early for retirement planning is a huge advantage, so you continue to add $50 every month. You do this for the next thirty-two years until your 50th birthday. Let's say the interest rate you earned annually was 5%. The total amount you've deposited is $19,700 (($50 x 12 months) x 32 years + initial $500 deposit). However, due to our good friend compounding interest, your investment is now worth $47,561.77!

I took our example and plugged it into an interest calculator at www.investor.gov. Below is a graph representing this example for the visual learner. The middle line is the assumed 5% interest rate. However, the top line represents a 7% annual interest rate. If that were the case, you would have almost $70,000! The bottom line on the graph represents a 3% rate. If you were to get that annual interest rate for thirty-two years, you would have a little over $30,000.

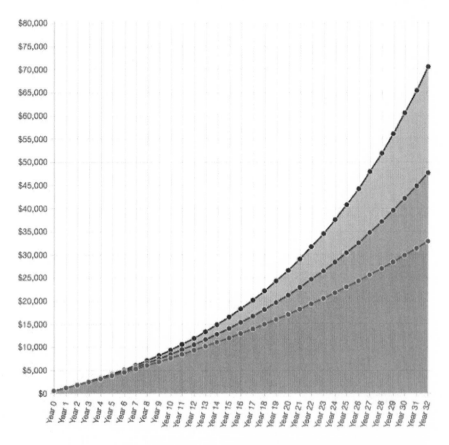

The take-home message here is to make a note of how powerful compounding interest can be. Remember, these numbers are based on investing $50 a month. That's pretty doable if you ask me! You can google "interest calculator" or use the same one I did and play with any numbers of your choosing.

Compounding interest is indeed a powerful force. The earlier you get started, the better off—and richer—you'll be. I can't stress this enough. Retirement may seem like a far-off destination for some of you, and it may be. However, it's absolutely necessary to understand the urgency in which you need to start saving now. As inflation and cost of living rise, the amount millennials and younger generations will need to retire also rises. According to CNBC, about 34% of millennials believe they only need $200,000 to retire comfortably. When in reality, that number is more like $1.18 million.[17]

Now you understand why you need to care about retirement. Let's look at a few different vehicles you can use to start saving today. Keep in mind that many retirement accounts are out there. However, keeping with the simplicity theme I've established throughout the book, I want to talk about three types: IRA (individual retirement arrangement), 401(k), and Healthcare Savings Account (HSA).

Different Account Types

Most people utilize two primary account types to help save for retirement: IRA and 401(k). These accounts share a few similarities. If you have an earned income, you can fund either of these accounts. Once you open one or both of these plans, you can't withdraw any money until you're 59 ½ years old without incurring a 10% penalty. However, you don't have to start withdrawing funds—often referred to as distributions—at age 59 ½. You can keep growing your account until you're 70 ½. At this point, you'll be required to take a minimum distribution. Both of these plans have contribution limits, meaning you can only contribute up to a certain amount annually. The contribution limits are different for each, so now is a good time to look at each plan a little more closely.

IRA

An individual retirement arrangement (IRA) is an appropriately named account that you can open to initiate retirement savings. IRAs can be opened through a financial institution or brokerage firm. It is important to note that an IRA is *not* an actual investment in and of itself. It is an account into which you deposit money to fund investments such as individual stocks, bonds, annuities, and mutual funds.** The institution at which you opened your IRA will manage your account. IRAs have a yearly maximum contribution limit. These limits can change or stay the same from year to year as cost of living adjustments are made by the IRS. For 2018, the maximum contribution is $5,500. However, if you're over the age of fifty, the IRS allows an additional $1,000 to be contributed as "catch up" since you're closing in on retirement. Despite the level of your contribution, your investments grow over time (hence why starting early is of great benefit). Because the money can be split up and allocated to different investments, your growth can vary year to year. This is why you can't simply ask the question, "What kind of return do I get for an IRA?"

Of course, risks come with investing in anything. Markets have highs just as they have lows. Some years will be better than others. In your younger years, you can afford to be more aggressive in the types of investments you have. As you age and get closer to retirement, you can transfer more of your money into safer investments, such as bonds. Another piece of advice would be not to make a habit of constantly checking your IRA. It'll drive you mad. If you happen to look at your account when the market is a bit rocky, you'll immediately want to sell everything to avoid further loss. However, it's better to let your account stand the test of time. Try to look at it maybe once a year. Leave the money alone and let it grow.

The beauty of an IRA is that it offers tax breaks. These tax breaks vary depending on the type of IRA you choose to open, which leads us to the two types of IRA accounts: *Traditional* and *Roth*.

With a traditional IRA, your money is placed into your account and invested. Remember, you have a $5,500 contribution limit. You don't have to fund it all at once nor do you have to fund the entire amount. Numerous options for amount and frequency of deposits can be discussed with your account manager. Depending on your income, your contributions are also tax deductible (lowers your overall taxable income). For a good reference to contribution limits and tax deductions, take a look at www.fool.com/retirement/2017/10/22/heres-the-2018-ira-contribution-limit.aspx.

Your account then grows tax-deferred. Over the years you have that IRA, you're not paying taxes on any of the money earned (gains). When you reach the point where you want to start using the money in your IRA, you'll pay taxes when the funds are removed. Remember, this will fall between the ages of 59 ½ - 70 ½. Therefore, since taxes are assessed when you withdraw, a traditional IRA would be beneficial for someone who anticipates being in a lower tax bracket when they retire.

A Roth IRA is practically the opposite of a traditional IRA. The money placed into a Roth IRA is *not* tax deductible. The benefit here is that this money grows *tax-free* and isn't taxed upon withdrawal in retirement. So, this account type is best if you think you'll be in a *higher* tax bracket in retirement.

Picture this. Say you've just graduated and scored your first entry-level job. Congrats! You're receiving an entry-level salary of $32,000. You love this industry and know you're going to do big things. You won't stop until you've made upper management. In this scenario, it would be wiser to invest in a Roth IRA because you more than likely will be in a higher tax bracket by the time you retire. Makes sense, right?

One last thing that should be understood about Roth IRAs is that they have income limits that will affect whether or not you can contribute. Depending on your income and how you file your taxes (single versus married filing jointly versus married filing separately), there's a chance you make too much money to contribute to a Roth. If that's the case, big baller, you can always contribute to a traditional IRA, as it has no limitations. You can look at a helpful chart regarding Roth IRA income limits by visiting www.fool.com/retirement/iras/2017/10/23/2018-roth-ira-income-limits-what-you-need-to-know.aspx.

401(k)

A 401(k) is named after the section of tax code to which it's referred (I know, it's riveting stuff). A 401(k) is the other most common type of retirement account. However, a 401(k) must be offered by an employer. This means you can't walk into a bank or brokerage firm and simply open a 401(k). Instead, you would have to opt-in or sign up for this through your employer, assuming one is offered, as it isn't mandatory. One of the great things about this being through work is that the contributions come directly out of your paycheck. Before you get all worked up over that idea, think about it for a moment. If you opt in from day one at your job, the money deposited into your account would never be missed. You wouldn't know what a paycheck looked like before that money went toward your 401(k).

Just as with an IRA, a 401(k) has a maximum contribution limit. For 2018, the limit is $18,500. Again, if you're over the age of fifty, the IRS allows for a "catch-up" contribution of an additional $6,000 making the limit $24,500.

A lot of companies will offer to match a certain percentage of your contribution. This is what makes 401(k)s so great! We can go back to our example used in the IRA section where you had recently graduated and landed a great entry-level job making $32,000/year. As you gained more experience, an offer from another company came along. They offered a $52,000/year salary and great benefits. Easy decision. You took the new job.

Part of these great benefits is that your new company will match up to 4% of your total contribution. This can sometimes be written as, "We will match 100% of your contribution up to 4%." This means that if you contribute 4% of your paycheck to your 401(k), your employer will *also* contribute the equivalent of that 4% (read: free money). So, you make $52,000/year. That comes out to $2,000 every paycheck (based on a biweekly pay period). Therefore, if you contribute 4% of your paycheck, you would be allocating $80 every pay to your 401(k), AND your employer would be matching that $80. You're essentially putting away $160 every single paycheck towards retirement—half of which is *free money*! I hope you can see how that adds up over time. Tis the beauty of an employer-matched 401(k).

Now if you're wondering, "Do they really just give me free money for contributing to a 401(k)?" The answer is yes and no. I promise this isn't going to be as confusing as that may have sounded. Please, bear with me. Often, with 401(k) plans, you'll see the term *vested* used. A company uses vesting to ensure you'll remain an employee of theirs for a specified time. Your employer will set a timetable until their matched contribution is vested. The money that they've matched will be yours after the designated time has passed. Using our example from above, suppose the benefits read, "We will match 100% of your contribution up to 4%, and you'll be vested after three years." In this example, all the money in your 401(k) is completely yours after three years. You should know that any money you directly contribute is always yours. If you were to leave this job after three years, you could take the entire amount with you. On the flip side, if you were to leave after a year, you could only take what you put in directly from your paycheck. You can see the incredible advantage that's there for the taking when you contribute to an employer-matched 401(k). Just make sure you know the terms when it comes to vesting. The last thing you would want to do is to take a new job and lose your employer-matched contribution because you left a month before you were vested!

Pro Tip: If you do decide to take a different job, you can roll over your current 401(k) into your new employer's 401(k) (assuming one is offered). You can do this by using a trustee-to-trustee transfer, which allows you to directly transfer your balance into the new account. This way, you avoid the 10% withdrawal penalty. Check out money.usnews.com/money/retirement/401ks with tips on how to roll over a 401(k)!

Just as with IRAs, a 401(k) can be traditional or a Roth. The Roth 401(k) is a newer investment strategy and may not yet be offered by your employer. However, it's becoming more and more commonplace. The major difference between the two again lies in the way taxes are paid. With a traditional 401(k), the money is placed directly from your paycheck into your account *before* taxes are paid on that earned income. This strategy helps lower your current taxable income, thus providing a bit of a tax break. Similar to a traditional IRA, your money grows tax-deferred until you want to withdraw funds. At this point, you'll pay taxes on the money that accrued over time.

A Roth 401(k) is similar to—yes, you guessed it—a Roth IRA in the sense that the money grows tax-*free*. However, with a Roth 401(k), the money placed in your account is post-tax. This means you paid taxes out of your paycheck before the money was placed into your 401(k). Upon retirement, you won't pay any taxes when you remove funds. The predominate deciding factor for which type of account you'll want to choose is the tax bracket you anticipate being in when you retire. However, if your employer offers both the traditional and Roth options, you don't have to choose between the two. If you're totally unsure of what tax bracket you'll fall in when you retire (I get it, it can be thirty or more years away for some of you), you can contribute to both and get the best of both worlds.

Generally, it makes sense for the younger saver to choose the Roth options (IRA and/or 401(k)) because, more often than not, as you age, you begin to earn more money, thus placing you in a higher tax bracket upon retirement. I realize that's not always the case and each of you should carefully contemplate where you think you'll end up in terms of income around retirement age. Ultimately, the decision is yours to make. It boils down to when you want to pay taxes, now or later.

HSA

Another account that can be used to save for retirement is the Healthcare Savings Account (HSA). This bad boy is a little-known gem and shouldn't be overlooked! An HSA is an account that can be used to save for medical expenses *and* reduce your taxable income. Think of it as a savings account, but you can only use the money for eligible medical expenses. In order to qualify for an HSA, you must be enrolled in a high-deductible health insurance plan (HDHP) on the first day of the month, not covered by another non-HDHP plan, not enrolled in Medicare, and not claimed as a dependent on someone else's tax return.[18] You can enroll through your employer if it's offered or through most financial institutions.

If you're enrolled through your workplace, you can set up pretax contributions to be deducted directly from your paycheck. If your account is through an institution other than your workplace, your contributions will be tax deductible since the money being deposited has already been taxed. The HSA also has a contribution limit. For the 2018 tax year, if you have single healthcare coverage, the maximum limit is $3,450. If you're enrolled in a family medical plan, the contribution limit is $6,900. An extra $1,000 can be contributed if you're age fifty-five or older.[19] The HSA separates itself from the IRA and 401(k) because you're not required to take any minimum distributions at a certain age (70 ½).

Once enrolled, you'll receive a debit card and/or checks that are linked to the funds in your account. You can then use your card or checks on any eligible medical expense, such as deductibles, copays and coinsurance, plus other medical expenses that may not be covered by insurance. An extensive list of qualified expenses can be found by going to www.investopedia.com/articles/personal-finance/090814/pros-and-cons-health-savings-account-hsa.asp.

At this point, you might be wondering, "What does a healthcare account have to do with retirement planning?" The answer lies within the tax advantages. Your contributions to an HSA are pretax/tax deductible *and* grow tax-free. Furthermore, when you withdraw funds for qualified expenses, you're not taxed on the money either! It's a triple threat tax advantage! Here's the catch: if you use the funds for anything outside of qualified medical expenses, you'll have to pay income tax and a 20% penalty. However, if you're sixty-five or older, you'll only pay the income tax. Generally, most of your healthcare expenses come in your later years. According to a CNBC article, a *healthy* sixty-five-year old couple that retired in 2017 will need roughly $275,000, in addition to insurance and Medicare, to cover healthcare costs while in retirement! [20] Who knows how much that number will increase by the time you retire. Therefore, it can be a huge advantage to have money set aside for any expenses that aren't covered by insurance or Medicare.

The most important concept I want you to take home from this chapter is that you need to start saving for retirement right now! Don't wait any longer! At the very least, get an account started. If you discover it's not the right fit for you, you can explore several options to roll one account over into the other, most of which don't have a penalty. I'm not asking you to change your life around here. Just throw a little money off to the side each month so you can continue to live that good life on into your golden years.

Chapter 10:

Social Insecurity

Social Security (SS) is a rather dense topic. As much as I don't want to bore you to death, I would be doing you a disservice to discuss retirement and not mention it. SS isn't the sexiest topic that anyone has ever written about, but It does play a large role in millions of Americans' retirement plans. However, I believe its benefits are often overestimated and not fully understood. Therefore, I'd like to take a little time to answer some of the following questions: What actually is Social Security? How do I qualify for it? When can I receive it? How much money do I get? Will it still be around when I retire? I know you're on the edge of your seat by now, so I'll cut right to it.

Social Security is a government program that was established in 1935 during the Great Depression. It offers financial assistance to people who are unable to work because they're old, disabled, or unemployed. The program requires workers to make regular payments to a government fund, which is used to make payments (benefits) to this population.[21] For the intentions of this book, I'm just going to focus on the money paid out during retirement.

In order to qualify to receive Social Security, you must work roughly 10 years and pay into SS through taxes on earned wages. In other words, a SS tax was taken out of your paycheck over those 10 years. If you never worked or worked for under 10 years, you can still receive SS benefits via your spouse. A *married* person is eligible to receive 50% of his or her living spouse's total benefit. A widowed spouse would be eligible to receive 100% of their deceased spouse's retirement benefits.[22] I would like the record to state that in no way am I suggesting that you kill off your spouse in order to receive SS benefits. It's not even that much money, guys; come on! Remember, I told you in Chapter 9 the average monthly SS check was $1,400 (or $350/week).

The timing of when you can receive the benefits from SS is where things get a little confusing. In general, everyone who meets the qualifying criteria is eligible to begin receiving SS at age sixty-two. However, just because you're eligible at sixty-two doesn't mean you have to start receiving benefits. There's a high likelihood you'd still be working and have a steady stream of income. Therefore, you wouldn't currently need the SS benefits and may choose to delay. Delaying until your full retirement age does have an upside that you'll see shortly. Regardless of when you choose to receive the SS benefits, they'll come in the form of a monthly payment from the government.

Here's where it can get a little tricky. The Social Security Administration (SSA) utilizes a concept called full retirement age (FRA). If you were born *after* 1960, your full retirement age is sixty-seven (yikes!). If you were born before 1960, you can visit www.SSA.gov for details concerning your FRA. At full retirement age, you'll receive the full amount (100%) of your earned SS benefit. It is possible, however, to start receiving SS benefits prior to your FRA. Although, you'll receive a lesser amount than if you were to wait until FRA (in other words, a lesser amount paid out over more years).

The rule of thumb when it comes to SS is the longer you wait to receive benefits, the higher the received monthly payment. If you're able to delay past your FRA, you can receive *over* 100% of your full retirement age benefit. For each full year you wait past your FRA, your benefit will increase by 8%. However, there is no advantage to delay past age seventy. Clearly, delaying isn't for everyone. If you choose to retire before your FRA, it's perfectly acceptable to receive your SS benefits. After all, you must generate a source of income. Although, we both know you already have an IRA and 401(k) to fall back on! Well done!

Not only does the age at which you elect to receive benefits affect how much your monthly payment will be, but the amount you've made over your lifetime also will be factored. Social Security monthly payments are also based on your 35 years of highest earnings. These don't have to be consecutive years. For example, if you switched careers midlife and started over at an entry-level job, those years wouldn't impact the prior years when you were most likely making more money. On the flip side, your job in high school waiting tables won't affect those numbers either. Unless, of course, you made more money in high school than you did in your adult years. In which case, you may have some other issues you might want to work out before worrying about retirement. Just saying!

In addition to deciding at what age you will receive your SS benefits, you must decide if you will continue to work once you start receiving them. If you take your SS benefits prior to FRA and continue to work, there can be advantages (increasing your 35 years of highest earnings and disadvantages (substantial withholdings from your SS check). However, if you take your SS benefits at FRA and continue to work, you are not penalized for your income (you will receive your full SS check), but you can be heavily taxed on your SS benefits. If you are interested in the fine detail I would recommend you go to https://www.fool.com/investing/2017/04/24/your-guide-to-working-while-collecting-social-secu.aspx

Let's look at an example to simplify this. Quick, fast-forward and you're age sixty-two—what a ride! Financially speaking, you have a lot of decisions to make. You're trying to decide if you should start receiving your SS benefits. While weighing your options, you remember reading this book and recall that I told you about full retirement age. You know that your FRA is age sixty-seven. You also remembered that I provided you this link, www.ssa.gov/planners/retire, to use in this exact situation. The SSA website offers an excellent chart breaking down how your SS benefits will be paid out depending on the age you choose to receive them. It's broken down month by month. If you choose to retire at sixty-two, you'll receive 70% of your total benefits; at age sixty-five, you'll get 86.7%; and at age sixty-six and 6 months—96.7%.

At some point, you've probably heard someone say that Social Security is eventually going to dissolve and won't be available to the younger generations. Let me shed a little light on this subject and clear the air. The short answer to the question of whether or not SS will still be around when millennials or generation Z begin to retire is: yes, it will be. However, there's something called the Social Security Trust. It was created at a time when the amount of taxes collected exceeded the benefits being paid out, creating a surplus. However, the days of the surplus are gone, and the SS program is only able to pay out about 3/4 of the total benefits. **The trust is now being used to make up the difference between the money coming in from SS taxes and the benefits being paid out.** The trust is currently projected to run out in 2034. At that point, the government will only be able to pay about 75-77% of the benefits assuming all other things remained equal (retirement age, benefit payments, taxes, etc.).[23] As you can see, the trust is moving toward depletion. Money is still coming in from taxes, as it always will. This should instantly make you realize that planning/saving for retirement is more critical than ever before! Again, remember that the average amount of a monthly Social Security check was $1,400 last year. If you're a millennial, imagine only getting 75% of that—about $1,050. Your savings and retirement accounts are going to be your nest egg. They're going to be what you'll fall back on, not Social Security. It would be best to consider SS as an added bonus but certainly not something on which you can solely rely.

My goal has been to show you why planning for retirement at an early age is paramount. If you're confident that you can live comfortably receiving roughly $1,000/month from Social Security, great! I wish I had your confidence! For those of us who feel otherwise, take the time to explore what retirement benefits your employer offers and research different IRAs. Start saving today!

When Can I Actually Retire?

You've just finished reading about full retirement age. You're well versed on that subject. Nevertheless, I want to pose a question you may not have considered yet. When can I *actually* retire? Intriguing, right? I hope so because this is where this book will change your life and the way you look at retirement! The best answer I've ever heard about when you can retire is when your *passive* income exceeds your expenses. Age isn't a factor!

By passive income, I'm referring to a situation in which you receive a stream of income without being actively involved, aside for the occasional contribution. It's easier to illustrate this with a few examples you probably encounter daily but maybe never thought about from this perspective. A great example is owning a rental property. Sure, when you first buy the property, you'll most likely have to put in some work. The same goes for when a tenant moves out. Compare that to all the months when you don't have to do much of anything, and those rent payments keep rolling in month after month! Here are a few other ways you can achieve a passive income:

- Create a blog
- Develop an app
- Write a book (haha, you caught me)
- Sell products on a site like Etsy or eBay
- Make YouTube videos
- Invest in dividend stocks

Your retirement accounts are also sources of passive income. Just remember that a 10% penalty is usually charged for withdrawing funds before the age of 59 ½. That's why it would behoove you to generate other sources of passive income and let these accounts grow while continuing to make regular contributions.

Pro Tip: If you want to start generating passive income but are stumped on where to start, try to think of times when people come to you for help. What are you good at? What types of situations do people ask for your advice or guidance? Jot down a few of those examples and start coming up with ways in which you can monetize them, a blog, a book, a physical product, etc. So many ways are available for earning passive income. Don't be afraid to get creative!

Generating multiple streams of passive income is an excellent way to supplement retirement accounts and Social Security. This is a concept I *never* learned throughout my years of education. I mention this because it is extremely difficult to estimate the amount of money you'll need in retirement. Expenses add up quickly. People tend to underestimate how much they'll actually be spending. As I've said before, no one wants to retire to a decreased quality of life by having to cut back on spending. These are your golden years! You want to travel while you can, visit family, or perhaps buy that house in Southern California you've always dreamt about.

It's almost impossible to determine how much money you'll need to set aside for things like healthcare costs or long-term care needs. I'm trying not to get too grim here, but no one knows how many years they're going to be living in retirement. Is it ten years? Twenty years? Thirty years? As you can see, there would be significant differences in the amount needed for ten years of retirement compared to thirty. Accordingly, let's look at ways you can save as much as possible.

Strategies to Save as Much as Possible

First, if your employer offers a 401(k) with matching, you need to be contributing at least as much as they'll match. If they match up to 4% of your contribution in full, you'd better damn well believe you're going to be contributing *at least* 4%. Again, that's FREE MONEY! It's a 100% return on your investment plus interest! Where else would you get that kind of return?

Now that you're getting the maximum contribution from your employer in your 401(k), I would recommend focusing on maxing out your IRA. Remember from Chapter 9, the most you can contribute to an IRA is $5,500 per year. This can be done all at once or over the course of the year. The maximum contribution for an IRA is much less than the max contribution of a 401(k)— $18,500. Therefore, you should try to contribute all you can to your IRA before returning to your 401(k) and increasing your contributions there.

If you're fortunate enough to contribute $5,500 to your IRA, then, by all means, increase your contributions to your 401(k)—if you're able to make it work within your budgeting. This is a good time to reiterate that all of this should be factored into the budgeting that you've done already. You shouldn't just begin to increase your retirement contributions before making sure you can make rent this month. A general principle regarding your 401(k) contributions is to try to increase it by 1% each year. Experts will commonly recommend that you should contribute anywhere between 10-15% of your gross income towards your retirement. However, there's no magic number I can tell you to contribute. Fortunately, most companies make it pretty easy to adjust your contributions. I would recommend playing with it a bit until you find what's comfortable for you. Nevertheless, **you should focus on paying off your outstanding debts *before* increasing contributions to your retirement account.** Priorities!

Retirement planning is so often overlooked and considered an afterthought. I hope the information I've given you has opened your eyes to the importance of starting early and taking advantage of your young age and compounding interest. Utilize your workplace's retirement benefits (if possible) and/or get started with your IRA. Social Security isn't something you can depend on by itself. It's never too early to start looking at ways to achieve passive income. And always remember, if you begin to accrue passive income and it exceeds your expenses, then, my friend, you can retire!

Chapter 11:

Taxes

April 15th can be one of the most dreaded days of the year, Tax Day! What can be more overwhelming than the possibility of owing the government thousands of dollars? Perhaps the lack of knowledge you have on the subject is even more crippling. "Oh, I owe an additional $800 to the government on top of the money I've already paid in taxes? Why don't you just rip my heart out of my chest while you're at it!?" These feelings can be all too real during tax season.

It's incredibly frustrating not to understand the process of filing your taxes. I remember the very first time I filed my taxes. I had no knowledge of how to file, what I needed, or how much I'd have to pay. You can bet I didn't even know online or e-filing was a thing. I gathered-everything I thought I might need and drove to the nearest H&R Block. Once inside, I sat one-on-one with an employee at a cubicle. I gave her my W-2 form and probably every identification you can imagine. You know, just to be safe. She then began banging away on her keyboard for what seemed like an hour. Who knows what she was actually doing. Was she preparing my taxes? Was she chatting on Facebook? Maybe she was booking a dinner reservation. Why was this taking so long? I was a single guy, barely making any money. There couldn't possibly be that much information to input. Finally, she was done and said, "Alright, it looks like you'll owe the federal government $110 and you'll receive $40 from the state."

What in the hell was going on? It already seemed as though I was giving 80% of my paycheck up in taxes. How could I need to pay even more!? I felt completely and utterly helpless. Right then, I vowed to learn more about taxes. I wasn't getting ambushed like this again. My first time filing was very traumatic, but yours doesn't have to be. Taxes don't need to be as complicated or mysterious as we make them, and I'm going to help you see that.

What Are Taxes?

Taxes are mandatory fees regulated by the federal and state governments. Both individuals and corporations are responsible for paying taxes. The most common types of taxes are income tax, sales tax, property tax, Social Security tax, and Medicare tax.

Income tax is a percentage of your income that goes to the state and the federal government. However, residents of certain states (Alaska, Florida, Nevada, New Hampshire, South Dakota, Tennessee, Texas, Washington, and Wyoming) don't pay a state income tax, only federal.

The amount you pay in taxes is determined by income tax brackets. Tax brackets are ranges of income that are taxed at different percentages. This is a progressive tax system. In other words, the amount of tax paid increases as your income increases. It's important to note that you're taxed on your adjusted gross income (AGI), not your gross income. Your AGI is your total income minus any qualifying deductions. Therefore, gross income is your overall total pay *before* accounting for taxes or other deductions. So, **when looking at the income tax brackets, remember to use your AGI, not your gross income**; otherwise, you'll overestimate the amount of taxes you owe. Let's not give the government any more money than we already do!

People often think that because you're in a certain tax bracket, you pay that percentage on all of your earned income, but for most, that's not the case. The tax rates are actually a tiered system. As you earn more and more taxable income, you progress through the tax brackets like a ladder. With each new step in the ladder, the tax rate increases. However, you're only taxed that rate on the income that falls within the bracket. Look at the 2018 federal income tax brackets in this chart:

Table 1: 2018 Federal Income Tax Brackets[24]

Tax rate	Single	Married, filing jointly	Married, filing separately	Head of household
10%	$0 to $9,525	$0 to $19,050	$0 to $9,525	$0 to $13,600
12%	$9,526 to $38,700	$19,051 to $77,400	$9,526 to $38,700	$13,601 to $51,800
22%	$38,701 to $82,500	$77,401 to $165,000	$38,701 to $82,500	$51,801 to $82,500
24%	$82,501 to $157,500	$165,501 to $315,000	$82,501 to $157,500	$82,501 to $157,500
32%	$157,501 to $200,000	$315,001 to $400,000	$157,501 to $200,000	$157,501 to $200,000
35%	$200,001 to $500,000	$400,001 to $600,000	$200,001 to $300,000	$200,001 to $500,000
37%	$500,001 or more	$600,001 or more	$300,001 or more	$500,001 or more

This seems more confusing than it needs to be so let's look at an example to break it down. Pretend your taxable income for the year was $50,000, and you're filing as single. According to the 2018 tax brackets, you fall within the 22% tax rate. However, you don't pay 22% on all $50,000 of your taxable earnings. Since the tax brackets are a tiered system, you would pay 10% tax on the first $9,525; 12% tax on the earned money between $9,526-$38,700; and 22% on the remaining $11,299.

Let's look at another example to ensure you get the gist of it. This time, let's look at Heather's situation. Heather is married filing jointly with her spouse. Together their combined taxable income is $170,000. Heather and her spouse are killing it! According to 2018 tax brackets, she falls in the 24% tax rate. She would pay 10% on the first $19,050; 12% on the income between $19,051-$77,400; 22% would be paid on the income between $77,401-$165,500; and 24% on the remaining $4,499. This progressive system ensures everyone starts at the lower tax rate and works their way up from there.

When it comes to state income tax, it can work one of three ways: either there is none, it's configured progressively similar to the federal income tax brackets, or there's a set percentage taxed on all taxable income. State income tax is largely dependent on the state you live in. Therefore, I would suggest that you check out TaxFoundation.org for more information on your specific state.

Most people are more familiar with sales tax because it is something they encounter daily. Sales tax is a tax you're charged when making most purchases. The rate of sales tax also depends largely on the state in which you live.

Property tax is a tax you pay on homes, businesses, and land you own. Similar to state sales tax, property tax also depends on the state and area in which the property is located. According to WalletHub, the average American household spent $2,149 on property taxes in 2017.[25]

FICA (Federal Insurance Contributions Act) tax is a tax not commonly considered by most. It's often referred to as Medicare and Social Security tax. Oh, did you think you were done with Social Security? I hate to be the bearer of bad news, but you can never escape it. As the saying goes, "Nothing in life can be said to be certain, except death and taxes."

Social Security tax is also referred to as Old Age, Survivors, and Disability Insurance. The SS tax is imposed on both employers and employees and is used to pay for retirement, disability, and survivorship benefits (widows and widowers). For 2018, SS tax is calculated as your gross earnings times 6.2% for W-2 employees and 12.4% for self-employed workers (1099). Currently, incomes over $128,400 that have already had the maximum SS tax of $7,960.80 withheld won't have additional withholding. The funds collected from employees for SS aren't put into the Social Security Trust we talked about in Chapter 10. Rather, they're used to pay existing retirees. Now you can see why I said the SS Trust is set to run out in 2034. We're not currently adding any additional funding to the trust. You're forced to pay into this program, even though there's no guarantee the trust will be around when you retire.

Medicare tax is smaller than the SS tax but doesn't have any contribution limits. Your Medicare withholding will include 1.45% of all your wages if you're a W-2 employee and 2.9% if you're self-employed. Additionally, an extra Medicare tax is levied for "high earners." Income over $200,000 for individual filers and $250,000 for married couples filing jointly will be subject to a 2.35% Medicare tax (1.45% regular rate + 0.9% high earner rate). This Additional Medicare Tax only applies to wages, compensation, and self-employment income over the $200,000 limit. It doesn't apply to net investment income.[26]

However, this doesn't mean investment income is safe from Medicare taxation. A Net Investment Income Tax (NIIT), also known as the Unearned Income Medicare Contribution Surtax, is added. This is a 3.8% Medicare tax that applies to investment income and to regular income over $200,000 for a single filer and $250,000 for married filing jointly. Examples of investment income that are subject to NIIT include dividends, interest, passive income, annuities, royalties, and capital gains.[26]

It's fun learning about all the ways in which you can get taxed, huh? It's cool if you want to grab another drink at this point. I won't say anything. Now that you've discovered even more ways in which the government takes your money, let's look at how it's actually done.

How Are Taxes Withheld?

At the start of any new job, you're asked to fill out an Employee's Withholding Allowance Certificate, or Form W-4 (unless you're self-employed or a contractor, which we'll discuss shortly). The first time I was presented a W-4, I had absolutely no idea what it was for or how to fill it out. Someone simply said, "Put single, claim zero allowances, and you're done." So, that's what I did. I still hadn't a clue what I just filled out, but that was one more piece of paperwork out of the way. This encounter may ring true for a lot of you, but the reality is, for something that so heavily affects you and *your* money, you really should understand the differences between IRS forms.

A W-4 is a form you complete at the start of a job or after a life event such as marriage or having children. As you know, the IRS requires you to pay taxes on your income. The W-4 indicates to your employer the correct amount of tax to withhold from your paycheck based on marital status and number of claimed allowances (exemptions). Accurately completing your W-4 is important because if too little tax is withheld, you could end up owing the IRS a big chunk of change come April. There's also a possibility you could owe interest or pay a penalty if too little is withheld. On the other hand, if too much tax is withheld, your paychecks won't be as large as they should be, and you'll get a refund check from the government in April. More on why that shouldn't be celebrated later in the chapter.

When you first start filling out the W-4, it's rather easy: name, address, and social security number. From there, it gets a little more confusing by asking about dependents, allowances, and marital status.

Dependents are children under the age of nineteen, disabled individuals, full-time students under the age of twenty-four, or elderly relatives who live with and are supported by the taxpayer. Under these criteria, the taxpayer can claim each as a dependent on their return.

A withholding allowance is an exemption that reduces the amount of income tax withheld from an employee's paycheck. The IRS suggests that you claim one allowance for yourself if you're not already being counted as a dependent on someone else's tax return. Claim another allowance if you're married and one for each of your dependents. This suggestion is meant to reduce the likelihood of owing money because of over-claiming allowances. Keep in mind, allowances and withholdings are inversely proportional. Here's an easy way to remember it: the more allowances claimed = less money withheld for taxes.

You'd think selecting your marital status would be the easy part of completing the W-4—not so much. You can choose one of three marital status options: single, married, or married but withholding at a higher single rate. That last option is also for people who are married filing separately.

At this point, you probably have a few questions. So, let me see if I can clear some of them up right now. Earlier, I mentioned I claimed zero allowances but proceeded to tell you the IRS recommends claiming one for yourself. So why would someone claim zero? For starters, it could be that the filer is a dependent on someone else's tax return. If they aren't a dependent, some will claim zero allowances to ensure the maximum amount is withheld from their paycheck. This is the best possible way to safeguard that they get a refund.

You may also be wondering why someone who's married would be filing to withhold at the higher single rate. Well, it's for the exact same reason. A single filer will have more money withheld from their paycheck than a married filer. Filing in this manner will ensure the highest amount possible is withheld to lessen the chance of owing the IRS. All of this is enough to make your head spin. Trust me; I've been there. Here's an example to help simplify:

Stephen and Lisa both have salaried positions where they make $60,000/year. They're paid every other week and, therefore, earn $2,308 each pay period. When completing their W-4s, Stephen claimed single with zero allowances (exemptions), and Lisa checked married with two allowances (her and her spouse). Using a federal payroll withholding calculator found at YourMoneyPage.com, we see that Stephen would have roughly $391.05[***] withheld in federal taxes per paycheck while Lisa would have only $213.66 withheld.

Pretend for a minute that Stephen instead claimed one allowance while Lisa kept her allowances the same (2) but chose married withholding at the higher single rate. Stephen would now have $352.10 withheld while Lisa's amount increases to $313.15. You can see that the single rate and fewer exemptions will result in the most money withheld from your paycheck.

As you learned in the above example, you can change your W-4 at any time to adjust your withholdings to suit your needs. If having more take-home pay is important to you, claim the appropriate number of allowances using the IRS strategy previously discussed. There's no limit to the number of allowances you can claim. However, don't just input a bunch of allowances because it could come back to bite you in the ass. You might end up owing a huge amount to the government in April and could possibly even face a penalty. Conversely, if you can't stand the thought of paying the IRS come tax season, then lower the number of allowances you claim in order to withhold more money from your paycheck. Check out www.calcxml.com/calculators/pay02 to get an idea of how changing your W-4 would affect your take-home pay and taxes withheld.

You now have a working knowledge that, sadly, many Americans don't have. Please understand that a W-4 is something you fill out, indicating how your taxes should be withheld; whereas, a W-2 is for your employer to complete at the end of the year. Let's now examine a W-2 more closely.

Your employer is required to provide you with a Wage and Tax Statement (Form W-2) from the previous year no later than January 31. Two important things should be noted here. First, if you're self-employed or an independent contractor, you won't receive a W-2. Instead, you'll receive what's called a Form 1099-MISC (pronounced "ten-ninety-nine" for short). Second, if you made less than $600 for the year, your employer may not be obligated to send you a W-2 or 1099.

A W-2 is divided into many different boxes containing information about your salary, Medicare, Social Security, and the amount of income tax withheld. Aside from making sure your social security number is correct, there's little you need to do with the W2 before filing your taxes. However, you should have three copies: one for your personal record, one to attach to your federal tax filing, and one to attach to your state tax filing. Although, if you plan to file online, one copy should be sufficient.

The 1099 form is an alternative to the W-2 form for self-employed, freelancers, and independent contractors. The 1099 is important to understand in our current society because many people are working for themselves or entering the "side hustle" game. Examples of those needing to utilize this form would be Uber drivers, freelance graphic designers, Airbnb hosts, Instacart shoppers, social media consultants, and many more who perform services for a company or individual but aren't direct employees. Look at it this way: W-2s are for employees while 1099s are for independent contractors.

When working as a W-2 employee, your taxes are automatically deducted from your pay. However, as a contractor (1099), you're responsible for estimating your own taxes and submitting them to the IRS quarterly. Don't be fooled by your first enormous paycheck as a 1099 contractor—no taxes were withheld! If you work a 1099 job and make more than $3,000 for the year, you should be submitting quarterly tax payments.[27] Therefore, if you find yourself in a 1099 position, it is very important to take a percentage of every paycheck and set it aside for taxes. If you don't do this, you can find yourself in a mess of trouble at the end of the year by potentially owing thousands of dollars to the IRS.

Pro Tip: If you envision yourself being self-employed or working as an independent contractor, it's a good rule of thumb to set aside 25-30% of each paycheck in order to pay quarterly taxes to the IRS.

Another form you should probably be familiar with is the 1098 (pronounced "ten-ninety-eight") form. A few different 1098 forms exist. For our purposes, you should be aware of the 1098-E and 1098-T forms. The 1098-E reports interest you paid on student loans. Most taxpayers are able to take a deduction on student loan interest. The 1098-T form is considered the "Tuition Statement." It reports how much you paid in tuition. Deductions can be claimed by most taxpayers on tuition-related expenses.

However, the 1098-T also reports any scholarships or grants you may have been awarded as they could reduce your overall deduction (subtracted from your tuition-related expenses).[28]

Dozens of tax forms are available on the irs.gov website. I wanted to touch upon some of the more commonly encountered ones. I hope you now have a better understanding of the use for all of these similarly named documents. So, let's move on to what you should do once you have all of these documents and are ready to file your taxes.

What to Know Prior to Filing

Prior to submitting your tax return, you need to choose your filing status, which includes five options: Single, Married Filing Jointly (MFJ), Married Filing Separately (MFS), Head of Household (HOH), and Qualifying Widow/Widower (QW). You may notice that these differ from the options available on the W-4. Remember, the W-4 is used to determine the amount withheld for taxes. Your filing status determines the amount of taxes you actually pay and the amount of your standard deduction. An important note: the IRS states that whatever your marital status was on the last day of the year, that's your marital status for the entire year.

The single status is used by unmarried people. This would include people who are divorced, *legally* separated, or cohabitating couples.

MFJ is typically used by most married couples. Although it isn't a requirement, MFJ usually provides more tax benefits than filing separately.

On the other hand, MFS usually provides the least amount of tax benefits. However, at times, MFS would be beneficial: one spouse may owe and the other may receive a refund, spouses are separated but not yet divorced, one spouse has a significant itemized deduction list, or you just wish to keep the tax liability separate. For example, if you knew your spouse was omitting income or claiming too many deductions, you could file separately in order to be responsible for just your return. It's worth mentioning if you're in this position, maybe now would be a good time to have a little sit-down with your spouse to discuss tax evasion and perhaps watch an Al Capone documentary.

If your spouse died during the tax year, you could still claim MFJ or MFS. However, for up to two years after the current tax year, you can claim QW, which gives you the same tax benefits and standard deductions as MFJ.

HOH is slightly more complex than the other filing statuses. When you file for HOH, you get a higher standard deduction and receive more tax benefits than the single status. Therefore, it's harder to meet all the criteria to qualify. The lure of a higher deduction and better tax benefits makes this the most erroneously filed status. In order to qualify, you must be unmarried, pay more than 50% of the cost to maintain your or a qualified person's home (mortgage, rent, utilities, etc.), and support a qualifying person.[29] That last part is where people can get confused. A qualifying person isn't the same as claiming a dependent. A qualifying person is a child, parent, or relative who meets certain conditions. Listing all of that criteria and having you read through it will surely put you to sleep. Instead, if you think you may qualify for HOH, then I highly suggest you look at ttlc.intuit.com/questions/2900097-what-is-a-qualifying-person-for-head-of-household to confirm whether or not you're eligible to file as HOH.

Remember, for a comparison of the tax rates for each filing status, refer to Table 1.

While reading this, you may find yourself unsure of which filing status to choose. Maybe you're married, and you and your spouse are uncertain whether to file jointly or separately. If you're filing online, you can always prepare multiple returns and file the one that saves you the most money (or refunds the most money). On the other hand, if a professional is preparing your taxes, they'll determine the best filing method.

Now that you know your filing status, there's some terminology you should be familiar with. By now, you've seen the term *taxable income* multiple times. If you recall, taxable income, or adjusted gross income (AGI), is your gross income minus qualifying deductions. Your AGI is the number used by the IRS to determine what you'll pay in taxes. Clearly, every working American would love this number to be zero. You might as well dream big! Meanwhile back in reality, others wonder, "How can I lower my taxable income?" Great question! Getting your AGI as low as possible is in your best interest.

When considering ways to lower your taxable income, *deductions* should be the first place you look. Deductions are usually everyone's favorite topic (if it's possible to have a favorite tax topic) because they help you save money. Who doesn't like that? Deductions are essentially work-related expenses, medical expenses, or charitable donations you've paid over the year. In the tax world, deductions are referred to as either standardized or itemized.

Standard deductions are the easiest to claim because you don't have to save receipts or have proof of expenses. The IRS, although hungry for your money, understands that you have to spend money to make money, so it sets a specific amount you can subtract from your yearly income; thus, reducing your AGI. For the 2018 tax year, the standard deduction is $12,000 for single filers, $24,000 for married filing jointly, $12,000 for married filing separately, and $18,000 for head of household.[§]

What does this all mean? As an example, let's say you're filing single. You made $40,000 gross income in 2018, and you choose to use the standard deduction. Therefore, you'll only pay taxes on $28,000 of your $40,000 yearly income because the standard deduction is $12,000. Sounds great, right? Not so fast! Sometimes, there's a better option, and that option is itemized deductions.

Itemized deductions are recommended over standard deductions if you've donated a large amount of money to charity, paid mortgage interest and property taxes, had large out-of-pocket medical expenses, or weren't reimbursed for job expenses. Clearly, for itemized deductions to benefit you, the amount of these expenses would have to be greater than $12,000—the current standard deduction amount. Another thing to keep in mind when calculating itemized deductions is that you need proof of your expenses. If audited, you'll be asked to show receipts or other documents to verify you had paid the expenses you're claiming. You want to make sure you have these documents before deciding to choose this option. Remember, you can't take both standard and itemized deductions; so, choose the one that will benefit you the most. To get a full list of eligible expenses that can be counted toward your itemized deductions check out the TurboTax blog.

Another important deduction that doesn't fall under the standard deduction category is student loan interest. This is one of those rare times where you can actually benefit from your student loan debt; so make sure you take advantage of it! To claim student loan interest as a deduction, you don't have to itemize. A separate category exists to which you can add the interest you've paid. The maximum amount you can claim is $2,500. You'll need to look at your end-of-year statement (1098-E) from your student loan company in order to see the shocking amount of interest you've paid. If the amount is under $2,500, then claim your exact number listed; if the amount is over $2,500, then claim $2,500.

Some exceptions apply for those who can claim student loan interest as a deduction. For example, interest from a Direct Plus Parent loan can't be used. Additionally, if, as a single filer, you've made over $75,000 for the year ($155,000 if you're married filing jointly), the government reasons you're doing very well for yourself and, therefore, shouldn't be able to claim student loan interest as tax deductible. You're also not allowed to claim student loan interest if someone is claiming you as a dependent on their taxes, such as your parents.

Another great way for lowering your taxable income is the use of an HSA. If you recall from Chapter 9, HSAs are either pretaxed directly from your paycheck or are tax deductible if you're contributing to an account you opened separately. Therefore, any of the retirement accounts we discussed are excellent ways to lower your taxable income. Don't be discouraged if you can't contribute to all of these accounts. Reread the strategy discussed in the retirement chapter and, at the very least, open one of these accounts and lower your taxable income!

Continuing in the spirit of saving money, let's discuss tax credits. A tax credit is something that lowers your total tax liability. That is, a tax credit lowers the actual amount of taxes you owe (after deductions). For example, you owe $2,000 in taxes but have a $500 tax credit. The amount of taxes owed is $1,500. Think of it as a really good coupon. Hence, you can see why the government doesn't give tax credits to just anyone.

Most tax credits are nonrefundable, meaning, they can't reduce the person's tax liability to below zero. For example, if you owe $500 in taxes but have a nonrefundable tax credit for $600, your amount owed would be zero instead of -$100. Ultimately, with a nonrefundable tax credit, the IRS isn't going to pay you the difference if it brings your balance under zero. Common nonrefundable tax credits are adoption tax credit, child tax credit (child under seventeen years old), foreign tax credit, and mortgage interest tax credit.

On the other hand, with a refundable tax credit, the IRS will pay you the difference if the value of the credit exceeds your tax liability. Using the same example from above, you owe $500 in taxes. However, this time you have a refundable tax credit of $600. The IRS will pay you $100. Win! Common refundable tax credits are the earned income tax credit, additional child tax credit, health coverage tax credit, and small business health care tax. For further information on tax credits, you can visit www.irs.gov. Lastly, for the sake of completeness, I should also mention that partially refundable tax credits exist, but that goes beyond the scope of this book.

Who Should File a Federal Income Tax Return?

Although it would be a dream never to have to file and pay taxes, the truth is that most people who earn an income must file a federal income tax return. Whether a person has to file a tax return is based on the following factors: age, marital status, annual income, and number of dependents.

The common answer to the question, "Who should file a federal income tax return," is anyone whose income is greater than the standard deduction, but what does this mean? As I've stated before, all nondependent taxpayers (not being counted as a dependent on someone else's tax return) are entitled to claim the standard deduction and a personal exemption. Fortunately for you, under the new 2018 tax plan, this is being simplified. For the 2018 tax year, the standard deduction amount has increased, and the personal exemption has been eliminated. Therefore, what you need to know is if a single filer's income is greater than $12,000, or a married couple filing jointly has an income greater than $24,000, you need to file a tax return.

Of course, you knew the answer wasn't going to be that cut and dry. You would also need to file a tax return if you made over $400 of self-employment, sold your home during that year, owe additional taxes on a retirement plan, or if you owe Social Security and Medicare taxes on income not reported to your employer, such as tips.[30]

Even if you're not required to file a return, you still may want to. For example, you can't receive a tax refund on withheld taxes unless you file a return. Additionally, if you're eligible to receive refundable tax credits, you can't receive these unless you file a tax return. This is important for nondependent students because you're eligible to claim a tuition and expenses credit up to $2,500—which for anyone living on Ramen, is worth taking the time to file.

Much of what I've told you so far has excluded dependents. To reiterate, a dependent is a person being claimed on someone else's tax return. This is typically true for disabled individuals, elderly relatives, children under the age of nineteen, or full-time students under the age of twenty-four. If you're a dependent, whether you're required to file a tax return is reliant upon earned income. Dependents who made more than $6,350 are required to file a return.[31]

Lastly, it would be advantageous to define taxable vs. nontaxable income briefly. Taxable items include wages; salaries; commissions; unemployment compensation; strike pay; rental income; alimony; royalty payments; stock options, dividends and interest; fringe benefits; and babysitting fees. As for monetary gifts, a single person can give another person $14,000 before it needs to be reported as taxable income. Therefore, a couple can give their child $28,000 without needing to report it to the IRS, or they could give their child and their spouse $56,000—that's a pretty lavish gift! Nontaxable items include things such as inheritances, gifts, and bequests; cash rebates on items you purchase; child support payments; most healthcare benefits; money that's reimbursed from qualifying adoptions; welfare payments; money someone leaves you through their life insurance policy; and scholarship money, unless used for room and board.[32,33]

If you're still unsure if you should file an income tax return, you can use this tool provided by the IRS at www.irs.gov/help/ita/do-i-need-to-file-a-tax-return to help guide your decision.

How to File Your Taxes

Now that you have the basics of the tax language down, you're ready to file your taxes! I'll pause a moment to allow you to regain your composure...

You have from January to April 15 to file and pay your taxes for the previous year. Before filing, be sure to collect all the appropriate documents you'll need: W-2s, 1099s, and any interest documents. Most of these things will either be available online or mailed to you by the end of January.

Once you've collected all your documents, you need to decide how you want to file. You may wonder if you should use an online software program or seek professional assistance. Some great online tax resources are available such as TurboTax and FreeTaxUSA. These websites can be fantastic for the average filer whose return is straightforward. However, if you find yourself with income from multiple sources or multiple states, you may want to seek the assistance of a professional.

The first step in filing your tax return is identifying which tax form you need to complete. The Form 1040 ("ten-forty") is the standard federal income tax form. It's referred to as "the long form" because it's longer and more detailed with its 79 lines. However, the 1040 can be useful to those who plan to claim numerous expenses, tax credits, and itemize deductions. In fact, if you plan to itemize your deductions, you *must* use this form.

A slightly simplified version of the 1040 form is the 1040A. To be eligible to use this form, an individual can't itemize deductions, own a business, or have a taxable income of more than $100,000. The 1040A limits tax deduction options to student loan interest, post-secondary tuition and fees, classroom expenses, and IRA contributions. Additionally, the 1040A also limits the tax credit options to the American Opportunity Tax Credit, Lifetime Learning Credit (LLC), Earned Income Credit (EIC), child tax and additional child tax credit, child and dependent care credit, credits for the elderly or disabled, and retirement savings contribution credit. Chances are, if you plan to take multiple tax deductions and/or credits, then you should use the regular 1040 form.[34]

The most simplistic form of the 1040 is the 1040EZ. This form is the fastest and easiest way to file an income tax return. However, in order to utilize the 1040EZ, you must meet the following criteria: you must have a taxable income less than $100,000, interest income less than $1,500, you can't be a dependent nor can you claim any dependents, and you can't itemize your deductions.[35] If you match this description, enjoy the 14 lines of bliss!

Once you determine the proper form you need, you can visit the irs.gov website and download the form from there. However, if you use an online program or hire a professional, their company will usually provide the form for you.

If you choose to hire a professional to do your taxes, you simply give them your documents, answer a few questions, and they prepare your taxes either right there or within a few days. These companies usually have the capability to submit your return online and will give you hard copies for your records. If you choose this option, you'll generally end up paying between $100-

$200 for their services. For some, the convenience is worth the price.

If spending between $100-$200 on taxes seems like throwing money away, I get it. Hopefully, you've already started your budgeting! In this case, you can choose to do your taxes online, which is relatively straightforward with most companies. TurboTax is one of the most well-known online tax software providers. I've personally used FreeTaxUSA for multiple years, and it has always been both easy to navigate and accurate. With a lot of these companies, you can file for free if you're using a 1040EZ or 1040A. If you're using a regular Form 1040, FreeTaxUSA is one of the few options that allow you to file your federal return for free. And at the time of writing, they're only charging $12.95 to file your state return. On their site, you can even upgrade to a deluxe version for an additional $6.99, which gives you the ability to live chat about questions you may encounter—a pretty great value for less than most spend at Starbucks.

If you decide to use an online program, they'll walk you through the process step-by-step. The following is a quick walkthrough of what you can expect to encounter on FreeTaxUSA. I use them as my example because I recently just filed my taxes using their website. I'm not even getting paid to push their services. It's just that easy!

To begin, you'll need to go to their website to register for an account and initiate the filing process. If you've collected all of the tax forms that pertain to you, the process will be straightforward. You'll be asked to input information from your W-2, additional wages, and IRA contributions. Next, you'll be asked to select which deduction—standard or itemized—is best for you. It will offer a recommendation based on information you input—a great feature if you're unsure which deduction to choose. Remember, you won't have to itemize in order to deduct your student loan interest. There will be a separate question pertaining to them so don't forget to take advantage of this option! Lastly, you'll be asked to input any tax credits for which you may be eligible. If you're wondering whether or not you qualify for credits, you'll have the option to answer a few questions to allow FreeTaxUSA to decide for you. And voila! Everything you learned has been put to use. Congratulations, you've filed your federal tax return!

Once you've completed your federal return, you'll be instructed to continue onto your state return unless you live where there's no state income tax. The state tax return is much shorter, and you'll simply input information as you did for the federal return.

Once your return(s) are completed, it's time for the moment of truth. You'll learn if you're receiving a refund or if you owe the IRS additional money. Owing money is never fun and is always a hard pill to swallow. Use the deductions to your advantage and take the time to learn if you qualify for any credits. Welcome to adulthood, where a lot of things just suck—especially taxes.

What to Know About Tax Refunds

Upon completion of tax preparations, most people anxiously wait to find out if they'll be receiving a big, fat refund check. However, as I've said so many times before, a large refund shouldn't be considered a good thing! Pump the brakes... Let me explain.

Receiving a refund means the government withheld too much of *your* money as tax payments. In other words, they took too much of your earned income. Essentially, you've given the federal government an interest-free loan. Think about that. Would they ever do such a thing for you? Hell no! That's money you could have contributed to your IRA, invested in some stocks or bonds, or even just money for that trip you missed with your friends because you couldn't afford it. Hence, if you're receiving a large refund, especially year after year, you should adjust your W-4. For example, if you're filing single with zero dependents, you should adjust to single and one or single and two. The closer you can get to breaking even when filing your taxes, the better. **If you only take away one thing from this entire chapter, *please,* let it be this.**

If you do find yourself getting a tax refund, you can expect to receive the money in about three weeks if filed online or six to eight weeks if filed by hard copy—one more perk of online filing. Another way to expedite the process is to receive your refund through a direct deposit setup, although this isn't an option if it's your first time filing a tax return. If you receive your refund via mail, you can expect it to take longer. However, there's good news for all those package-tracking addicts out there! The IRS has an app you can download and track your refund. Happy tracking!

A refund isn't the only thing that can happen post-filing. The IRS can also audit you for that year or up to six previous years. If audited, the IRS will send you a mailed letter. Remember, the IRS always first contacts you by mail, *never by phone.* If you've received phone calls claiming to be the IRS and demanding payment, they're always scams—so be cautious. If audited, the IRS may request additional information about certain items shown on the tax return such as income, expenses, and itemized deductions. According to USA Today, less than 1% of people are actually audited. The odds do increase, however, for the higher income earners. Earners making more than $200,000 have about a 1.7% chance of being audited. If you make $1 million or more, you're facing a 5.8% audit rate.[36]

The IRS may also notify you that there's an error or multiple errors on your tax return. If this happens, you'll need to file a 1040X. If you had your taxes done by a professional, you should notify them right away and ask to have your taxes redone—for free. If you prepared the refund yourself, you may want to consider seeking assistance from a professional to avoid facing extra costs or penalties.

What if I Can't Pay My Taxes?

Unfortunately, some of you may ask yourself this question. Tax season is approaching, and you suspect you'll owe the IRS money. Yet you know you won't be able to pay. Take a deep breath. Options are available for you, but you still need to file a tax return on time to avoid further penalties. The first option is to contact the IRS to discuss payment options. The IRS may be able to provide you with options such as short-term extensions, payment plans, or a settlement amount. However, keep in mind that the IRS is always going to charge you interest on the money you owe. Lending money interest-free is one-sided in your relationship with the IRS. Alternatively, you may be able to pay with a credit card. This would only be a desired route if you *absolutely* know you'll have the money within a month or two. Damaging your credit and the card's high interest rates can be catastrophic. **I don't recommend this option.**

That's it for taxes folks! This is probably the toughest section to make it through, so great job, and thank you! It's a difficult concept to understand fully. I recommend using this chapter as a guide. Make notes or highlights and come back to it whenever you need, like tax season. I hope I've helped alleviate some of the stress that can come with filing taxes. Armed with this information, you no longer have to dread April 15th—or, at least, not for lack of knowledge.

.

Chapter 12:

Conclusion

Phew! I know; that was a lot of information in such a short time. But that was my intention. I want you to finish reading this book so you can get out there and apply these concepts. I didn't want you spending weeks reading a tome and forgetting mostly everything by the time you finished. Therefore, let's do a quick recap of what you've learned.

You've seen how easy budgeting your money can be. Budgeting shows where you can afford to make adjustments and save more money than you ever thought possible. You've learned about high-yield savings accounts and the higher interest you can earn compared to traditional savings accounts. You're now aware of how your credit score is built. You learned how to properly manage your credit cards and reap the rewards they can offer. Managing your debt will be a breeze now. You understand that you need to pay off your debts with the highest interest rates first. There's a light at the end of the tunnel regarding paying off your student loans. You've learned how to consolidate and refinance them, which can ultimately save you thousands of dollars over the years. You've seen the importance of starting your retirement savings right now. Take advantage of your employer's match to your contribution on your 401(k). Open an IRA if you're able. Use your youthfulness to your advantage and watch your money grow leaps and bounds! Taxes shouldn't scare you anymore. You now know why you have certain amounts of money withheld from your paycheck and can adjust your W-4 as needed. You should understand that it's not a great thing to receive large refund checks after filing your taxes. And never forget—if you reach a point where your passive income exceeds your expenses, you can retire. All and all, you've become financially educated!

These are the basic building blocks of personal finance. Certainly, a lot more is out there that I didn't touch upon. However, understanding these concepts will give you the confidence in knowing you can become financially free! Debt doesn't have to hold you down any longer. Your credit score and savings will skyrocket. Your student loans will dwindle away. You'll be able to retire comfortably because you started saving when you were young and knew what you were doing. Taxes are inevitable and will follow you everywhere. That's just the truth. However, there's no reason that should add anxiety to your already busy life. You now have a better knowledge of taxes than most people. You got this!

We often encounter stressful financial situations every day. The preceding information is intended to make life a little easier by eliminating that stress. By understanding these basic financial concepts, you can now be confident in your fiscal decisions. The struggle is over! As I mentioned at the beginning of the book, money makes the world go 'round. Controlling your finances gives you the freedom to control your world. So, go out there and enjoy what the world has to offer!

Lastly, if you have any questions or just want to say what's up, please don't hesitate to email me at Brandon@strugglehood.com. Thanks again for reading! #strugglehoodended

Disclaimer

This book and its content are for personal use only and are protected by applicable copyright laws. The content of this book is intended to be used for informational purposes only and should not, under any circumstance, be interpreted as providing, or used for personal investment, tax, or legal advice. This book and its content should further not be considered an offer to sell, the solicitation of an offer to buy or sell, or investment advice pertaining to the buying and/or selling and/or holding of any security, credit card, loan program, or any other financial instrument.

The author of this book is not a licensed or registered financial or investment advisor, or securities broker, and is not otherwise by any means licensed or authorized to provide financial, investment, or wealth management advice. All opinions, analytical conclusions, and other content set forth herein are those of the author and are not intended nor should be interpreted as financial, personal investment, or wealth management advice. All such opinions and other content set forth herein are based on reliable and reputable sources and have been written in good faith. This book and its content are not to be interpreted as a representation or warranty, expressed or implied, of any kind, to warrant or otherwise guarantee the accuracy and/or completeness of the information set forth herein, or to otherwise warrant or guarantee the performance of any current or future security, loan program, credit card, investment strategy, or financial and/or wealth management program.

The author has not and will not accept any liability in connection with the use and reliance of this book and its contents to make personal financial planning and management decisions, or to invest in current or future securities. Any reference to a third party or third-party products and/or services included herein shall

Please Help!

Thank you for reading my book!

I hope I was able to enlighten you on a few financial concepts and provide some relief from financial stressors in your life. I would absolutely love to hear your feedback. It would mean the world to me if you'd leave an honest review on Amazon letting me know what you thought of the book. The only way I can make appropriate updates and become a better writer for future projects is to learn from your feedback. Thank you so very much!

Endnotes

1) Long, Heather. "Sex Ed Is Required. Why Isn't Financial Education?" *CNN, Cable News Network*, 4 Sept. 2016, www.cnn.com/2016/09/04/opinions/sex-ed-is-required-but-not-financial-education-heather-long/index.html. Accessed February 18, 2018

2) Issa, Erin. "NerdWallet's 2017 Household Debt Study." *NerdWallet*, (n.d). www.nerdwallet.com/blog/average-credit-card-debt-household/. Accessed February 18, 2018

3) Huddleston, Cameron. "More Than Half of Americans Have Less Than $1,000 in Savings in 2017." *GOBankingRates*, 19 Sept. 2017, www.gobankingrates.com/saving-money/half-americans-less-savings-2017/. Accessed February 18, 2018

4) Kadlec, Dan. "Bold New Rule: Students in the U.K. Must Study Personal Finance." Time.com, *Time*, 14 Feb. 2013, business.time.com/2013/02/14/bold-new-rule-students-in-the-u-k-must-study-personal-finance/. Accessed February 18, 2018

5) Ranzetta, Tim. "What Actions Are Countries Taking to Improve Financial Education?" NGPF Blog, *Next Gen Personal Finance*, 6 June 2017, www.ngpf.org/blog/policy/actions-countries-taking-improve-financial-education/. Accessed February 19, 2018

6) Tierney, Spencer. "Best High-Yield Online Savings Accounts of 2018." NerdWallet, 19 Dec. 2017, www.nerdwallet.com/blog/banking/best-high-yield-online-savings-accounts/. Accessed February 14, 2018

7) Staff, Investopedia. "Credit." *Investopedia*, 16 Jan. 2015, www.investopedia.com/terms/c/credit.asp. Accessed January 15, 2018

8) Dilworth, Kelly. "Rate Survey: Average Card APR Remains at 16.15 Percent." CreditCards.com, 21 Nov. 2017,

www.creditcards.com/credit-card-news/interest-rate-report-112117-unchanged-2121.php.). Accessed January 15, 2018

9) Bar, Cecilla. "Types of Student Loans." *Debt.org*, (n.d.). www.debt.org/students/types-of-loans/. Accessed January 31, 2018

10) "Repayment Plans." *Federal Student Aid*, 7 Dec. 2017, studentaid.ed.gov/sa/repay-loans/understand/plans. Accessed January 31, 2018

11) McGurran, Brianna, and Teddy Nykiel. "How to Consolidate and Refinance Your Student Loans." *NerdWallet*, 20 Oct. 2017, www.nerdwallet.com/blog/loans/student-loans/consolidate-student-loans-2/. Accessed February 1, 2018

12) Sourmaidis, Demetrios. "Public Service Loan Forgiveness Information & Eligibility Assessment." *Student Debt Relief | Student Loan Forgiveness*, 24 Nov. 2017, www.studentdebtrelief.us/forgiveness/public-service-loan-forgiveness/. Accessed February 3, 2018

13) Hess, Abigail. "Here's What Happens if You Don't Pay Your Student Loans." *CNBC*, 15 Aug. 2017, www.cnbc.com/2017/08/15/heres-what-happens-if-you-dont-pay-your-student-loans.html. Accessed February 3, 2018

14) Fay, Billy. "Paying Student Loan Debt: Modification & Repayment Options." *Debt.org*, (n.d.). www.debt.org/students/what-to-do-if-you-cant-pay-your-student-loans/. Accessed February 4, 2018

15) "Deferment and Forbearance." *Federal Student Aid*, 19 Oct. 2017, studentaid.ed.gov/sa/repay-loans/deferment-forbearance#forbearance-eligibility. Accessed February 4, 2018

16) Campbell, Todd. "How Big Is the Average Person's Social Security Check?" *The Motley Fool,* 30 Aug. 2017, www.fool.com/retirement/2017/08/30/how-big-is-the-average-persons-social-security-che.aspx. Accessed January 25, 2018

17) Elkins, Kathleen. "Here's How Much Millennials Think They Need to Retire-and How Much They Actually Need." *CNBC,* 17 Jan. 2018, www.cnbc.com/2018/01/16/how-much-money-millennials-think-they-need-to-retire.html. Accessed January 25, 2018

18) Folger, Jean. "Pros And Cons of a Health Savings Account (HSA)." *Investopedia*, 17 Nov. 2017, www.investopedia. com/articles/personal-finance/090814/pros-and-cons-health-savings-account-hsa.asp. Accessed March 5, 2018

19) Martin, Ray. "IRS Allows Higher Retirement Savings Account Limits for 2018." *CBS News,* CBS Interactive, 24 Oct. 2017, www.cbsnews.com/news/irs-allows-higher-retirement-savings-account-limits-in-2018/. Accessed March 5, 2018

20) Grant, Kelli B. "Expect to Spend More on Health Care in Retirement — Even if You're Well." *CNBC*, 24 Aug. 2017, www.cnbc.com/2017/08/24/average-couple-will-spend-275000-on-health-care-in-retirement.html. Accessed March 7, 2018

21) Social Security. (n.d.). *Merriam-Webster.* www.merriam-webster.com/dictionary/social%20security. Accessed January 28, 2018.

22) Carlson, Robert C. The New Rules of Retirement: Strategies for a Secure Future. John Wiley & Sons, Inc., 2016.

23) Max, Sarah. "Will Social Security Really Run Out of Money?" *Money,* 21 Mar. 2016, time.com/money/4213065/will-social-security-run-out-money/. Accessed January 20, 2018

24) Orem, Tina. "2017-2018 Federal Income Tax Brackets." *NerdWallet*, 25 Jan. 2018, www.nerdwallet.com/blog/taxes/federal-income-tax-brackets/. Accessed January 21, 2018

25) Kiernan, John S. "2017's Property Taxes by State." *WalletHub*, 1 May 2017, wallethub.com/edu/states-with-the-highest-and-lowest-property-taxes/11585/. Accessed January 21, 2018

26) Josephson, Amelia. "What Are Medicare Taxes?" *SmartAsset*, 15 Dec. 2017, smartasset.com/taxes/what-are-medicare-taxes. Accessed January 21, 2018

27) Zulliger, Laura. "How to Calculate and Pay Quarterly Estimated Taxes." *Payable*, 9 Sept. 2015, payable.com/blog/calculate-pay-quarterly-taxes. Accessed January 29, 2018

28) TurboTax. "Guide to 1098 Tax Forms." *TurboTax Tax Tips & Videos*, Jan. 2017, turbotax.intuit.com/tax-tips/home-ownership/guide-to-1098-tax-forms/L8s74M2aZ. Accessed March 1, 2018.

29) "Do I Qualify for Head of Household?" *TurboTax Support*, Intuit, 8 Nov. 2017, ttlc.intuit.com/questions/1894553-do-i-qualify-for-head-of-household. Accessed March 3, 2018

30) "Do I Need to File a 2017 Tax Return?" *Efile.com Taxes Made Simple*, (n.d.). www.efile.com/tax/do-i-need-to-file-a-tax-return/. Accessed January 29, 2018

31) IRS. "Who Must File." *Publication 501: Exemptions, Standard Deduction, and Filing Information*, Department of the Treasury, p. 4, www.irs.gov/pub/irs-pdf/p501.pdf. Accessed January 29, 2018

32) TurboTax. "Taxable Income vs. Nontaxable Income: What You Should Know!" *TurboTax Tax Tips & Videos*, (n.d.). turbotax.intuit.com/tax-tips/irs-tax-return/taxable-

income-vs-nontaxable-income-what-you-should-know/L0h4j5DZQ. Accessed January 29, 2018

33) Herigstad, Sally. "Gift Tax: Do I Have to Pay Tax When Someone Gives Me Money?" *TaxAct Blog*, 3 Jan. 2018, blog.taxact.com/gift-tax-do-i-have-to-pay-gift-tax-when-someone-gives-me-money/. Accessed January 29, 2018

34) Momoh, Osi. "1040A Form." *Investopedia*, 2 Oct. 2017, www.investopedia.com/terms/1/1040a.asp.   Accessed January 30, 2018

35) Erb, Kelly Phillips. "A Beginner's Guide to Taxes: Which Tax Form Should I File?" *Forbes*, 21 Feb. 2013, www.forbes.com/sites/kellyphillipserb/2013/02/10/a-beginners-guide-to-taxes-which-tax-form-should-i-file/#71ae08c03515. Accessed March 4, 2018

36) McCoy, Kevin. "Your Odds of Facing an IRS Audit Are 1-in-143." *USA Today*, 6 Mar. 2017, www.usatoday.com/story/money/2017/03/06/your-odds-facing-irs-audit-1--143/98808612/. Accessed January 31, 2018

* For simple math purposes, this example assumed interest was compounded only once a year. In reality, the interest would more than likely be compounded monthly and your accrued interest would be even higher.

** Specific types of investments are beyond the scope of this book. So, I won't dive into that. Who knows, maybe that will leave room for my next book?

*** It should be noted that for the purpose of this example, no pre-tax deductions (retirement plan contributions, healthcare, dental, vision, etc.) were taken into consideration. For simplicity, state taxes were not calculated.

§ The new tax legislation passed at the end of 2017 has drastically changed the standard deduction numbers that will be used in this book. Also, note that when I say the 2018 tax year, I'm referencing the time when you're filing your taxes in 2019 for your earnings from 2018.

Acknowledgements

I want to thank my wife, Niki. Without her, this book wouldn't exist, and chances are, I'd be lying face down in a drained pool somewhere. You've been my editor, my proofreader, my copywriter, my designer, and my inspiration when I was struggling. You kept me going and made me a better writer. I love you!

I certainly want to thank my father, Bill Brumage, for his input and grammatical wizardry. Your early childhood teachings of "home row" and "asdf jkl;" have finally paid off!

A big thanks to Joe Carter for his dedication to helping a friend out in any way possible. Everyone would be lucky to have someone like you in their corner. Thank you!

I'd also like to thank Brian Nickerson for his wisdom and guidance through the legal world that continues to baffle me. Thanks also to Kim Boggs, JD Lister, Justin Kline, and all the other respondents that helped with my research and questionnaires. Shout out to all the people who have helped launch this book. Your passion and hard work is truly amazing!

Lastly, I want to thank *you* for reading this book and taking a chance on a first-time author. It means so much to me that you were willing to sit down and let me into your life for a little while. I hope this book was able to help you in some way.

About the Author

Brandon is a first-time author living in Chicago, IL with his wife and two cats. However, he grew up in West Virginia where he attended West Virginia University and Saint Vincent College in Latrobe, PA. He may not live there anymore, but he will always have a passion for WVU and Pittsburgh professional sports teams. He currently works as a Certified Registered Nurse Anesthetist (CRNA) in Chicago.

Brandon realized that a generation of adults were not properly taught personal finance. Through personal experiences, awkward situations, dedicated research, and lengthy interviews and discussions, Brandon wrote his first book that you have before you. His goal is to make personal finance a subject that's enjoyable and easy to learn.

Check out his website, strugglehood.com, for new and updated material or shoot him an email at Brandon@strugglehood.com to get in touch! And, of course, don't forget to follow the Strugglehood Facebook and Instagram pages:
Facebook: facebook.com/strugglehood
Instagram: @strugglehood

Made in the USA
Middletown, DE
20 July 2018